PASTA

Anne Ager

PASTA

WARD LOCK LIMITED · LONDON

© Ward Lock Limited 1984

First published in Great Britain in 1984
by Ward Lock Limited, 82 Gower Street,
London WC1E 6EQ, a Pentos Company.

Text filmset in Linotron Goudy
by HBM Typesetting, Chorley, Lancs.
Printed and bound in Italy by Sagdos SpA

British Library Cataloguing in Publication Data

Ager, Anne
    Pasta—(Ward Lock cookery course)
    1. Cookery (Macaroni)
    I. Title
    641.8'22   TX809.M17

    ISBN 0-7063-6309-4

CONTENTS

Acknowledgements
Photography by Edmund Goldspink
Home economist   Jacki Baxter
Stylist   Emma Hartley

The author and publisher would like to thank the following
companies for sponsoring photographs:
Corning Ltd (page 34); Lamberti Wines (page 38);
Mushroom Growers Association (page 30); New Zealand
Kiwifruit Information Bureau (page 74) **and** Pasta Pasta
(page 46).

The author and publisher would also like to acknowledge
the following companies for kindly loaning equipment for
photography:
Bella Figura, Ceramic Tile Design, David Mellor,
Divertimenti, Richard Dare **and** Sloane Square Tiles.

Fresh pasta and olive oil on page 46, all ham, salami,
cheeses and Amaretti provided by Pasta Pasta.

Pasta for all other photography provided by the Pasta
Information Centre.

Notes
It is important to follow *either* the metric *or* the imperial
measures when using the recipes in this book. Do not use a
combination of measures.

All recipes serve four people, unless otherwise specified.

INTRODUCTION

The origins of pasta are steeped in myth and legend, and there is much controversy as to where it actually originated. Some people believe that the Arabs introduced pasta to the island of Sicily during the twelfth century. Others, however, hanker after the Chinese theory; it is purported that one of Marco Polo's men (named *Spaghetti,* no less!) stole the recipe for pasta from a Chinese courtesan, and brought it to Europe.

The Italians are passionate about pasta; they feel almost as strongly about pasta as they do about opera, so it is hardly surprising that they have a museum in Pontedassio dedicated to this emotive, staple food. Anyone who visits the museum, as I did several years ago, will be able to look through ancient documents, which clearly state that pasta was being eaten and enjoyed as early as 5000 BC.

Wherever the real truth lies, it is an indisputable fact that for the last two or three centuries, Italy has been the true home of pasta. Many other countries now consume pasta in quite substantial quantities, but they will never quite match the Italians at what is after all 'their own game'. Italian pasta dishes captivate the vibrant and colourful character of the country and its people: the rich deep flavours from herbs and pungent cheeses; the fruitiness of sun-ripened tomatoes and peppers; the round smooth characteristic flavour and heady aroma of virgin olive oil; and a certain robustness from wines, Marsala, plump black olives, and the all essential garlic!

It is hoped that this book will bring a ray of Italian sunshine into your kitchen, so that you, your family and friends can share some of the delicious pasta dishes that have their roots in Italy.

WHAT IS PASTA?

Pasta is derived from wheat – one of the world's natural foods. The endosperm, or centre kernel of the wheat grain, is ground to a fine semolina and then mixed with water to a firm, smooth dough. Other ingredients such as egg and oil may also be added. Each variety of pasta has its own particular texture, dependent upon the amount of water and other ingredients within the dough. It is at this stage that the consistency of the final dough is regulated. For example, if oil is incorporated it will give a dough with a greater elasticity than one without oil.

Top quality commercially manufactured pasta is made from prime durum wheat, whereas the lesser quality pastas are made from a blend of cheaper wheats. The latter type of pasta is often soft and sticky once cooked. Durum wheat pasta, however, has a firm texture with 'a bite' to it, and the cooked pasta has a characteristic nutty flavour. How to tell? Most fresh pasta is made from durum wheat; if you are buying dried pasta; carefully check the ingredients listed on the packet.

The next stage in the making of commercial pasta is the shaping; the kneaded dough is rolled out or extruded through shaped moulds known as dies, giving each particular type of pasta its characteristic shape. Pasta is still quite moist and pliable at this stage, and is sold either fresh or dried in boxes or bags. Dried pasta has been allowed to dry thoroughly in a carefully controlled temperature. Additionally, some commercial pastas are sold either frozen or canned.

For home-made pasta, see page 16.

NUTRITIONAL VALUE

Pasta is not the fattening food that it is sometimes thought to be; an average portion, about 50g/2 oz dried weight, amounts to about 837 kiloJoules/200 calories. The best quality pasta is a good source of protein and is considerably more nutritious than other 'starchy' foods such as potatoes, bread and rice. Wholewheat pasta is, additionally, a good source of natural fibre as it is less refined than pasta made from white flours.

The Varieties of Pasta

The pasta family is a large and varied one; it is not only the shape that differentiates one variety from another, but also the colour and texture. Pasta is coloured naturally; yellow pasta is plain pasta without any colouring, and the deeper the colour, the more egg it contains. Green pasta gets its colour and characteristic flavour from fine spinach purée. Orange pasta contains tomato purée, and brown pasta is made from wholemeal or wholewheat flour.

The Italians have such a wide range from which to choose that they could eat a different type on each day of the year. In most other countries the selection of pasta is more limited, but the many varieties are becoming more readily available.

Most of the pasta that is eaten outside Italy is bought in its dry, packeted form, but the availability of fresh pasta is increasing rapidly. Many supermarkets sell fresh pasta as do some speciality shops that are devoted almost exclusively to pasta in its diverse forms. Such pasta takes less time to cook, but is in every other way similar to dried pasta.

Pasta falls into three principal categories – long pasta, such as spaghetti and fettucine; shaped or short pasta such as rigatoni, twistette and farfalle, and sheet pasta, the only variety of which is lasagne. Stuffed pasta such as ravioli and cappelletti, tend to be regarded as a category on their own, but are usually grouped together with the short or shaped pastas.

Listed below are some of the most readily available varieties of pasta outside Italy. The same variety is sometimes known by more than one name, depending on the pasta manufacturer and its country of origin, so the following list only acts as a descriptive guide.

The pasta types are, incidentally, interchangeable within each category so that, for instance, bucatini can be substituted for spaghetti, if liked. Some pastas are, however, more practical to use for certain dishes than others. Generally speaking, long pastas are served with a topping sauce or are gently mixed into the sauce; shaped pastas are more robust and are mixed into their sauces while flat pastas are used for layering and baking. The smaller pasta shapes are most used in soups as they do not hold sauces well.

Category	Description	Availability
LONG PASTAS		
Bucatini	Thinner than spaghetti but not as thin as *spaghettini*	Dried
Capelli d'angelo	The thinnest of the long pastas – a very fine vermicelli, often referred to as 'angel's hair'	Dried
Fettucine	Very fine noodles, almost rod-shaped	Fresh and dried
Fusilli	Twisted spaghetti, wider than the standard spaghetti	Dried
Gemelli	Rope or plaited spaghetti	Dried
Maccheroni	The general name given to long tubular macaroni. Other shapes are sometimes also called *maccheroni*	Dried
Pappardelle	The fattest of noodles; much thicker than tagliatelle	Fresh and dried
Spaghetti	The most popular pasta. Long thin tubes of pasta available in different diameter strands	Fresh and dried
Spaghettini	The thinnest of *spaghettis*	Fresh and dried
Tagliatelle	Long ribbon noodles, wider than *fettucine*, but not as fat as *pappardelle*. Cut white noodles are often referred to as *nouilles*	Fresh and dried
Vermicelli	Very thin spaghetti, but not as thin as *Capelli d'angelo*; it usually comes curled into clusters or strands	Dried

Category	Description	Availability
SHAPED PASTAS		
Anelli	Ring-shaped pasta; the little rings are called *anellini*	Dried
Anellini rigati	Ridged, ring-shaped pasta	Dried
Cannelloni	Although this usually comes under the category of 'shaped pasta', it is actually made from flat or sheet pasta, formed into large hollow pasta tubes	Fresh and dried
Conchiglie	This is the term generally used for all shell-shaped pastas. Sizes vary somewhat, and the tiny shells are known as *conchigliette*	Fresh and dried
Ditali	A form of cut macaroni, shorter than *elbow maccheroni*, and sometimes called *thimble macaroni*	Dried
Elbow maccheroni	Curved short lengths of macaroni; even the Italians refer to it as elbow maccheroni	Dried
Farfalle	Butterfly or bow-shaped pasta; the smallest ones are called *farfallette*; the slightly larger size *farfalline*, and the largest butterfly pasta *farfalloni*	Dried
Lumache	Medium-sized snail-shaped pasta	Dried
Lumachine	Small pasta snails	Dried

Chart continues over.

Category	Description	Availability
Orzo	Small pasta shapes resembling plump long-grain rice	Dried
Penne	Diagonally cut tubes of pasta, cut from tubular macaroni	Dried
Rigatoni	Large ridge-shaped pasta tubes	Fresh and dried
Stelline	Small star-shaped pasta	Dried
Twistette	Stubby spirals of pasta	Fresh and dried

SHEET PASTAS

Lasagne	Completely flat sheet pasta	Fresh and dried
Lasagne riccie	Rippled sheets of *lasagne*	Dried

FILLED PASTAS

Agnolotti	Half-moon *raviolo*	Dried
Cappelletti	Pasta shaped into 'little hats', and stuffed with a savoury filling	Fresh and dried
Ravioli	Squares of pasta sandwiched with a savoury filling	Fresh and dried
Tortelline	Small twists of pasta stuffed with a savoury filling	Fresh and dried

Although most of the pasta types mentioned above are fairly widely available outside Italy, there are within Italy itself distinctive preferences for certain varieties according to region. Generally, the South tends to favour ready-made packeted spaghetti and noodles, whereas the Northern Italians prefer the shaped pastas, especially the shaped and filled varieties such as ravioli.

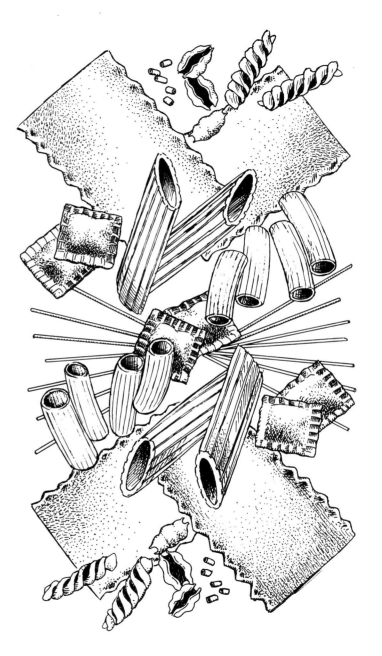

Storage of Pasta

Fresh/Dried	Cooked/Uncooked	Storage Life	Freezing
COMMERCIAL PASTAS			
Fresh pre-packed	Uncooked	Use by 'best by' date	Pack in easily usable quantities in polythene bags, excluding air. Twist tie and freeze for 6 months. Cook from frozen.
	Cooked	Overnight only	Undercook slightly, drain, cool and pack in polythene bags. Store for 1 month only. Put into boiling water, bring back to boil and cook for a few minutes until *al dente*.
Freshly made	Uncooked	Wrap in clingfilm and store in a refrigerator for 48 hours	As commercial fresh
	Cooked	Overnight only	As commercial fresh
Dried	Uncooked	6 months – unopened 2 weeks – opened	— —
	Cooked	Overnight only	As fresh
Commercially frozen	Uncooked	—	Store for 1 month only. Cook from frozen, following manufacturer's instructions.
	Cooked	Overnight only	As commercial fresh
HOME-MADE			
Fresh	Uncooked	Overnight only	As commercial fresh
	Cooked	Overnight only	As commercial fresh

THE FLAVOURS OF PASTA COOKING

The style of cooking varies very much from one part of Italy to another, and the dishes not only reflect locally available produce, but also the prosperity of the particular region. The most marked difference is that between the North and South of the country; the North of Italy is generally more wealthy, and the people eat a lot of meat, dairy produce and egg-enriched pasta. The Italians in the South, however, exist on a more economical diet, yet it is none the less colourful – locally produced olives and olive oil, fish which is abundant in the coastal regions, home-made goat cheeses and manufactured pasta.

Italian pasta dishes echo these regional characteristics, but they also encapsulate the overall colour, aroma and flavour of a wide variety of Italian produce. It is these ingredients which lend that very authentic flavour to pasta – glossy red and green peppers, and bright purple aubergines; juicy citrus fruits (oranges, lemons and limes); a wide variety of fresh herbs, such as basil, oregano, thyme and parsley; spices such as coriander, saffron and ginger; and the two most important ingredients in any Italian kitchen – olive oil and garlic.

Olive oil is used extensively in pasta dishes, both for tossing the cooked pasta and for preparing the sauces. Use a good quality olive oil wherever possible, as it makes a great deal of difference to the flavour.

Garlic is the other main-stay of pasta cooking, but for some people it is an acquired taste. If you only like a subtle garlic flavour, then use a bruised clove which can be removed easily; if, however, you prefer a stronger more traditional flavour, crush or finely chop the garlic before adding it to the pasta sauce (this will vary according to the particular recipe).

Fresh herbs make an enormous difference to the final flavour of a pasta dish, and it is worth all the effort involved in obtaining them. Several fresh herbs can be bought from most good supermarkets and many greengrocers. If you find these difficult to obtain locally, then you can use one-third the quantity of the equivalent dried herb. Basil is the most widely used herb in Italian cooking, not just for pasta, but it is also one of the most difficult to grow; it does not like cold climates, and the specially cultivated and imported varieties tend, therefore, to be fairly expensive. Even so, it is worth remembering that for most dishes you only need about three leaves which means that any you do not use can be frozen. With spices, it is advisable to buy the whole varieties, and crush or grind them as required; the dried, ready prepared ones tend to lose their characteristic flavour very quickly.

Cheese and pasta are particularly complimentary to one another, and the appropriate variety of cheese is normally chosen very carefully. The very hard Italian cheeses, such as Pecorino and Parmesan, are finely grated and usually used to sprinkle over cooked pasta dishes; they are sometimes also used in the preparation. The softer, easy-melting cheeses, such as Bel Paese, Fontina and Mozzarella are frequently added to made-up pasta dishes prior to cooking, such as Lasagne al Forno (see page 34).

Tomatoes are another important Italian ingredient. The big mis-shapen Mediterranean tomatoes have a much fuller sweeter flavour than the average-sized regular tomato. If you find these difficult to buy, you can always use good quality canned ones. Many tomato-based sauces are served with pasta, and the canned ones drained in water rather than in fresh tomato juice, are excellent for such sauces – drain well before using.

Most cooked pasta dishes comprise a sauce, either as a serving accompaniment or as part of the made-up dish. Tomato sauces have already been mentioned, but a very classic Italian pasta sauce is Pesto; it can be bought either ready-made from most good supermarkets, alternatively you can make your own at home (see page 65).

Wine and Marsala are essential ingredients in many pasta sauces; they contribute a fullness of flavour and a native robustness.

Freshly ground black pepper may sound a very basic ingredient, but I have intentionally extracted it from the other pasta flavourings. Several pasta dishes are very simple in make-up, yet it is the careful and distinctive seasoning that completes the finished dish. Salt is important, but for really good pasta, black pepper is an absolute must.

The popularity of pasta has created both an extension and a development in its uses. The USA, for instance, is particularly keen on pasta salads – both simply prepared side salads with dressings and vegetables – and more substantial salads made with fish or meat which serve as main-course dishes.

PASTA AS MAMA MAKES IT!

Fresh pasta has already been mentioned, (see page 8) and nothing quite beats the home-made article. Most Italian mamas have developed a strong right arm over the years, from kneading endless batches of pasta dough, and it is a time-consuming and demanding job. The satisfaction of kneading pasta by hand is very similar to the feeling achieved when making home-made bread. For those who do not feel up to the rigours of pulling and punching pasta dough, there are several short-cuts. The basic dough can be made in a food mixer fitted with a dough hook, or in a food processor fitted with a paddle blade; this eliminates the pulling and punching by hand. Alternatively, it is possible to buy small machines that will actually make the pasta dough as well as shaping it. They do, however, tend to be quite expensive, but are worth purchasing if you plan on making a lot of pasta. If it is the shaping of the actual pasta that worries you, then there are many gadgets to come to your aid, ie a hand operated pasta machine, which will cut noodles (eg fettucine and tagliatelle) and sheet pasta of different widths at the turn of

a handle, a noodle 'wheel' which can be run along the full length of the rolled out pasta dough, and a ravioli mould.

Home-made pasta is not difficult to make, but you do need to be patient and have plenty of time. If you are a gifted bread and pastry maker, then you will find it extremely easy.

Making pasta at home can be a messy business and you need to allow yourself plenty of room; you can use a very large chopping board or a marble slab, or alternatively, you can roll out the prepared dough on a clean kitchen work surface. If you are rolling the dough by hand (and not by machine), then an extra long rolling-pin is particularly useful.

Pasta is best made from a good strong flour (one that has plenty of gluten content) so that the dough will roll and stretch readily. It is not essential to add eggs to a home-made pasta dough, but it does make it more easy to handle and shape, especially for first time makers. Although the quantity of oil used is relatively small, it is important that it should be olive oil; other oils will not give such a good flavour.

A selection of equipment for making different types of pasta

PASTA ALL'UOVA
BASIC PASTA DOUGH – ENRICHED WITH EGG

Makes 450g/1lb

This dough can be used for making all types of pasta.

450g/1 lb strong plain flour
1 × 5ml spoon/1 teaspoon salt
4 eggs, beaten
1 × 15ml spoon/1 tablespoon olive oil

Sift the flour and salt into a mound on a clean work surface. Make a well in the centre, then add the eggs and olive oil. Gradually draw in the flour from the edges and work together to a smooth dough. Knead vigorously on a well floured surface until firm, very smooth and elastic. (This can be done in an electric mixer or food processor as mentioned on page 14). You should be able to stretch the kneaded dough without its surface cracking and crazing. This will take about 20 minutes, depending on how practised you are at kneading, and whether you do it by hand or by machine. Cover the prepared pasta dough with a damp clean tea-towel and leave it to relax for 30 minutes.

Divide the dough into two or three portions, depending on how much space you have. Roll each portion of dough out very thinly on a floured surface, lifting it from time to time to ensure that it is fully stretched and has not stuck. The secret of really good home-made pasta is to get it rolled out extremely thinly; you should be able to lift the rolled dough up to the light and see dark objects through it!

Sheets of lasagne are usually cut by hand to suit the size of the dish to be used. For fettucine or tagliatelle, hang the rolled sheets of dough on a clean floured tea-towel, over the back of a chair. Leave to relax for 10 minutes, then roll the sheets of dough up loosely, as for a Swiss roll. Using a very sharp knife, cut the roll of pasta dough at regular intervals, to give even-sized strips – 5mm/¼ inch for fettucine, and 1.25cm/½ inch for tagliatelle. (If you have a pasta shaping machine, you can regulate the thickness of the dough by adjusting the numbered dial close to the turning handle; the rolled dough can then be fed back into the machine and cut into noodles, either the size of fettucine or tagliatelle.)

The shaped pasta can either be cooked immediately or it can be hung over the back of a chair on a clean tea-towel and left to dry for 1–2 hours.

Variations

Wholewheat Pasta
Use 100g/4oz wholewheat flour and 350g/12oz strong plain flour. Make as for Basic Pasta Dough.

Pasta Verde
Add 3–4 × 15ml spoons/3–4 tablespoons sieved cooked spinach to the flour, eggs and olive oil when working to a smooth dough.

Ravioli
Roll out the prepared pasta dough as thinly as possible into four even-sized rectangles. Place small spoonfuls of filling 4cm/1½ inches apart in straight lines on two sheets of the dough. Run a dampened pastry brush in straight lines between the filling, then lay the two remaining sheets of pasta over the top of each filled sheet. Press down firmly between each mound of filling to seal the two layers of dough. Cut the ravioli into 5cm/2 inch squares by running a pastry wheel or sharp knife in straight lines along the pressed areas. Separate the squares of ravioli and use as required.

If you have a simple hand ravioli mould (this looks rather like an ice-cube tray), roll out the prepared pasta dough as thinly as possible. Lightly grease the mould and lay a sheet of rolled dough over it; press it carefully into each indentation. Brush the raised areas of dough, between the divisions, with water or beaten egg. Put a small spoonful of filling into each indentation, then lay another sheet of rolled dough over the top. Roll across the top of the mould with a short rolling-pin to sandwich the filling between the two layers of dough and to divide it into small squares of ravioli. Use as required.

Alternatively, ravioli can be prepared using a special rolling-pin with notched squares on its surface. The ravioli squares are formed by rolling the pin over the pasta.

Another way of preparing ravioli is by using a special attachment to a standard pasta shaping machine, as for other pasta types.

For the filling, use either a very thick Bolognese Sauce (see page 29) or a mixture of half cooked spinach, well drained, and half ricotta or sieved cottage cheese.

Other Home-made Shaped Pastas
Roll out the prepared dough as thinly as possible and prepare your own shapes, eg bows, twists, etc.

COOKING, SERVING AND EATING PASTA

Pasta is a very simple food to cook, but it does not always receive the careful attention which it deserves. It is very easy to ruin if not cooked correctly, and few things are less appetizing then soggy, overcooked pasta. Whether you are cooking fresh or dried pasta, the same general rules apply; only the length of cooking time varies.

1) Bring a large solid-based pan of water to the boil, allowing approximately 2.4 litres/4 pints water per 350g/12 oz pasta.

2) Add 1×15ml spoon/1 tablespoon olive oil and 1×5ml spoon/1 teaspoon salt to the pan as the water comes to the boil. The oil prevents the pasta from sticking and the salt will bring out the essential flavour of the pasta.

3) Lower the pasta into the pan carefully, keeping the water on the boil. For long pasta, such as spaghetti, 'curl' it gradually around the inside of the pan; add short pasta in spoonfuls to the boiling water. Slide large pasta such as lasagne into the water individually to prevent the sheets sticking together; count 10 between each addition.

4) Stir the pasta *once* only to separate the individual strands or shapes. Do not stir any more otherwise starch is released unnecessarily and this will affect the final texture of the pasta.

5) Cook at a rolling boil until the pasta is just *al dente* (ie firm to the bite).

Suggested cooking times for principal pasta types

Pasta type	Fresh	Dried
Spaghetti	3 minutes	8–9 minutes
Fettucine	2–3 minutes	5–10 minutes (according to make)
Tagliatelle	2–3 minutes	5–10 minutes (according to make)
Pasta shapes (eg farfalle, conchiglie, etc)	2–3 minutes	6–8 minutes
Filled pasta (eg ravioli etc)	3–4 minutes	6–8 minutes
Vermicelli	—	1–2 minutes
Lasagne	— (pre-cooking)	6 minutes (pre-cooking)

Note The cooking times of other pasta types can be determined by comparing their size with some of those listed above.

6) To test, take a little of the pasta from the pan and bite it; it should be firm to the tooth yet tender (ie *al dente*).

7) Drain the cooked pasta thoroughly in a large sieve or colander. Do not rinse pasta.

SERVING AND EATING PASTA

The Italian approach to serving and eating pasta is very different to that in many other countries. In Italy, pasta is often served as part of a complete meal, in fact as a separate pasta dish. This is not to say that pasta is never served as the sole dish of a meal with a simple salad or two.

It is a common mistake to serve pasta in portions that are too large; this is why it has inherited the reputation for being over-filling and fattening. Pasta should be served to enhance the appetite and not to discourage or dampen it, and you should be able to leave the table afterwards without feeling over-full.

As a general guide, allow approximately 50g/2oz pasta (uncooked weight) per person for a starter or dessert and 75g/3oz pasta (uncooked weight) for a main course. Heavily sauced, very rich pasta dishes are best reserved for serving as a main meal with a salad, whereas simple pasta dishes are perfect to start a meal. Pasta salads can be served as a course in their own right. Allow about 75g/3oz pasta (uncooked weight) per person for a simple salad and 40–50g/1½–2oz pasta (uncooked weight) for a more elaborate salad with added protein or one to be served as a starter. Alternatively, a selection of different pasta salads can be served with salamis and other Italian cold meats as a mixed hors d'oeuvre. Soups do not require more than about 20g/¾oz pasta (uncooked weight) per person.

Serve cooked pasta piping hot and serve made-up pasta dishes, such as lasagne, on pre-warmed plates. Accompanying salads are always served in separate bowls or on small side plates so that the temperature of the pasta does not wilt the salad. Make sure that the ingredients used in a side salad complement those used in the pasta dish, ie, if the flavour of the pasta and its sauce are fairly strong, keep the salad very simple, with a reasonably bland dressing.

There is an art in eating long pasta, such as spaghetti and tagliatelle, which is why many people would prefer not to eat it in public; they would prefer to make a fool of themselves in the privacy of their own homes. The Italians, however, are nowhere near as self-conscious; they have few inhibitions, and many of them look positively barbaric when eating pasta, using their forks like shovels and their noses touching their food! It is an art that is so simple to master, that there need never be any embarrassment. Children nearly always manage to make a mess when eating pasta, however good their table manners, and it is a good idea to tie a large napkin around their necks before they start eating.

The implements needed for eating pasta are minimal; some people like to use a spoon and a fork, but a fork is all that is really necessary for long pasta, pasta shapes and even made-up pasta dishes. Stick the prongs of your fork into the long pasta, and twist it round and round until you have a manageable mouthful. Lift the fork up from your plate, allowing any loose strands of pasta to drop off, and pop the forkful quickly into your mouth.

FOR PASTA PROFESSIONALS

I came back from my last visit to Italy with the most wonderful gadget; a special pasta fork! It looked just like any other fork, apart from the fact that there was a small turning handle set into the end of the wooden fork handle. You push the prongs of the fork into a portion of long pasta, and, holding the fork steady, you rotate the turning handle; it automatically winds the pasta around the prongs of the fork. Perhaps a gimmick, but very successful!

PASTA SOUPS

Italian soups are often served as a complete meal, and this is why so many contain pasta – usually a small shaped pasta. Thin soups generally have their pasta cooked in them while thick soups use pasta which has been cooked separately so that the pasta is not lost in the natural thickness of the soup.

Pasta soups do not necessarily need an accompaniment, but most people find them rather 'naked' eaten on their own. Crusty Italian-style bread is perfect, or you can, of course, serve grissini and a bowl of tangy grated cheese, such as Parmesan or Pecorino.

Stock is a very important ingredient in all soup making, and home-made stock is always preferable. There are recipes in this chapter for Brodo di Pollo (chicken stock) and for Brodo di Manzo (beef stock), both of which are simple to prepare and make a vast difference to the finished dish.

BRODO DI POLLO
BASIC CHICKEN STOCK

Makes 1.8 litres/3 pints stock

1 large boiling chicken
1 veal shank (225g/8 oz approx)
3.6 litres/6 pints water
2 large carrots, roughly chopped
1 large onion, roughly chopped
2 sticks celery, chopped
2 bay leaves
a bunch of parsley stalks
a few sprigs rosemary
1 × 5ml spoon/1 teaspoon crushed peppercorns

Put the chicken into a large pan with the veal shank and the water, and bring to the boil slowly. Remove any surface scum with a perforated spoon. Add the remaining ingredients and bring back to the boil, then cover, reduce the heat and simmer gently for 2½–3 hours.

Strain the prepared stock through a piece of clean muslin or cheesecloth. Store, covered, in a refrigerator for up to 4 days.

Variation
To serve the stock as a clear soup, clarify it first. Put the strained stock into a clean pan and add two crushed egg shells and two stiffly beaten egg whites. Bring to the boil, stirring all the time, then strain again through clean muslin or cheesecloth.

Cook pasta in the cleared soup.

Brodo di Manzo
BASIC BEEF STOCK

Makes 1.8 litres/3 pints stock

900g/2 lb beef bones
3 medium carrots
2 medium onions
3.6 litres/6 pints water
450g/1 lb shin of beef, roughly chopped
2 sticks celery, chopped
a small bunch of parsley stalks
2 bay leaves
1 × 5ml spoon/1 teaspoon crushed peppercorns
1 × 2.5ml spoon/½ teaspoon crushed mustard seed

Put the beef bones, carrots and onions into a roasting tin, and bake in a hot oven, 200°C/400°F/Gas 6, for 30 minutes until really well browned.

Put the browned bones, carrots and onions into a pan and add the water. Bring to the boil slowly, then remove any surface scum with a perforated spoon. Add the remaining ingredients and bring back to the boil. Cover, reduce the heat and simmer gently for 3 hours.

Strain the prepared stock through a piece of clean muslin or cheesecloth. Store, covered, in a refrigerator for up to 4 days.

Variation
Clarify as for Brodo di Pollo (page 19).

Zuppa di Broccoli alla Romana
BROCCOLI SOUP

2 × 15ml spoons/2 tablespoons olive oil
1 large onion, finely chopped
50g/2 oz Parma ham, cubed (see **Note**)
1 large clove of garlic, crushed
1.2 litres/2 pints Brodo di Pollo (chicken stock, page 19)
225g/8 oz broccoli, broken into florets
salt, freshly ground black pepper
50g/2 oz stelline (small pasta stars)
50g/2 oz Parmesan cheese, grated

Heat the oil in a large pan. Add the onion and Parma ham and cook gently for 4–5 minutes, then add the garlic and chicken stock. Bring to the boil, then reduce the heat and simmer for 10 minutes.

Meanwhile, blanch the broccoli by simmering the florets in boiling salted water for 5 minutes. Drain thoroughly and add to the stock with the stelline. Season to taste with salt and pepper, then simmer the soup for 2 minutes until the pasta is tender. Serve in warmed soup bowls and sprinkle each portion with grated Parmesan cheese.

Note Small cubes of Parma ham can be bought from many good delicatessens and supermarkets, at a much cheaper price than the sliced variety.

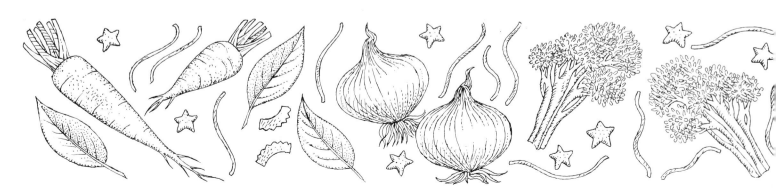

PASTA E FAGIOLI
PASTA AND BEAN SOUP

175g/6 oz dried white haricot beans
1 large onion, sliced
2 large carrots, sliced
2 stalks celery, sliced
1 large clove of garlic, finely chopped
1 small ham bone
2.4 litres/4 pints Brodo di Pollo
(chicken stock, page 19)
100g/4 oz elbow maccheroni
2 × 15ml spoons/2 tablespoons olive oil
50g/2 oz Parmesan cheese, grated
2 × 15ml spoons/2 tablespoons chopped parsley
salt, freshly ground black pepper

Soak the beans for 8 hours or overnight in cold water. Drain them, then put into a large pan with the onion, carrots, celery, garlic, ham bone and chicken stock. Bring to the boil, then reduce the heat and simmer gently until the beans are tender. Drain off about half the cooked beans from the soup and pass them through a sieve. Remove the ham bone and trim off any small pieces of meat. Return the sieved beans and chopped ham to the soup and bring back to the boil. Add the maccheroni and simmer steadily for 2–3 minutes until the pasta is tender. Stir in the oil, grated cheese, parsley and seasoning to taste. Serve piping hot in warmed soup bowls.

RAVIOLI IN BRODO
CHICKEN AND RAVIOLI SOUP

1.5 litres/2½ pints Brodo di Pollo
(chicken stock, page 19)
4 × 15ml spoons/4 tablespoons chopped parsley
175g/6 oz fresh ravioli
salt, freshly ground black pepper

GARNISH
× 15ml spoons/4 tablespoons olive oil
4 × 15ml spoons/4 tablespoons stale coarse breadcrumbs
1 small clove of garlic, crushed

Put the chicken stock into a large pan and bring to the boil. Add the parsley and ravioli, and bring back to the boil. Reduce the heat and simmer steadily until the ravioli is just tender.
　Meanwhile, prepare the garnish. Heat the oil in a pan and fry the crumbs and garlic until crisp and golden.
　Season the soup to taste, and serve in warmed soup bowls. Sprinkle with the fried breadcrumbs.

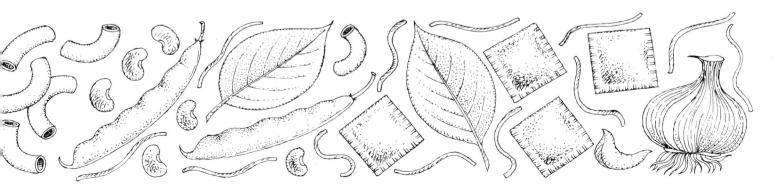

ZUPPA DI POMODORO CON POLPETTINE
TOMATO SOUP WITH MEATBALLS AND PASTA

1 slice of white bread, 1.25cm/½ inch thick, broken
into large pieces
4 × 15ml spoons/4 tablespoons milk
50g/2 oz butter
1 large onion, finely chopped
225g/8 oz lean veal **or** pork, finely minced
1 × 5ml spoon/1 teaspoon chopped fresh sage
salt, freshly ground black pepper
a generous pinch of ground nutmeg
2 egg yolks
2 medium carrots, grated
675g/1½ lb Mediterranean tomatoes, skinned, de-seeded
and chopped
1 clove of garlic, crushed
1 litre/1¾ pints Brodo di Manzo (beef stock, page 20)
450ml/¾ pint dry white wine
75g/3 oz vermicelli

Mix the bread with the milk, then leave to stand for 10 minutes.
Squeeze the bread to remove excess moisture. Melt 25g/1 oz of
the butter in a pan and gently fry half the onion until soft. Mix
with the squeezed bread, the minced meat, sage, seasoning to
taste, nutmeg and egg yolks, and mould into small balls about
the size of an olive. Chill for 30 minutes.

Meanwhile, melt the remaining butter and fry the remaining
onion for 3–4 minutes. Add the carrots, tomatoes, garlic, beef
stock and wine, and bring to the boil, then reduce the heat and
simmer for 45 minutes.

Press the soup through a sieve into a clean pan. Bring the
soup back to the boil and add the prepared meatballs. Reduce
the heat and simmer gently for 12 minutes, then add the
vermicelli and simmer for a further 2 minutes. Adjust seasoning
to taste. Serve the soup in warmed deep soup bowls.

MINESTRA DI VERDURA
VEGETABLE AND HAM MINESTRONE

2 × 15ml spoons/2 tablespoons olive oil
50g/2 oz pork **or** ham fat, chopped
1 large onion, finely chopped
2 large carrots, chopped
3 sticks celery, chopped
100g/4 oz spinach, shredded
100g/4 oz green cabbage, shredded
salt, freshly ground black pepper
3 × 15ml spoons/3 tablespoons finely chopped parsley
1 × 15ml spoon/1 tablespoon chopped fresh marjoram
175g/6 oz piece bacon **or** gammon, skin removed
1 small pig's trotter
1.8 litres/3 pints Brodo di Pollo
(chicken stock, page 19)
75g/3 oz nouilles (broken noodles)

Heat the oil in a large pan, add the chopped fat and cook until
the fat runs free. Add the onion, carrots and celery, and fry
gently for 5 minutes, then add the remaining ingredients apart
from the noodles. Bring to the boil, then reduce the heat and
simmer for about 45 minutes until the bacon and meat on the
trotter are tender.

Remove the piece of bacon and the trotter from the soup.
Chop the bacon and remove the meat from the trotter bone in
small pieces. Add the chopped meats to the soup. Bring the soup
back to the boil and add the broken noodles. Stir steadily for
2–3 minutes until the pasta is tender. Serve the soup in large
warmed soup bowls.

Zuppa di Pomodoro con Polpettine

Minestra di Crostacei
LOBSTER AND TOMATO MINESTRONE

1 medium lobster, cooked
1 litre/1¾ pints water
salt, freshly ground black pepper
50g/2 oz butter
1 small onion, finely chopped
450g/1 lb Mediterranean tomatoes, skinned,
de-seeded and chopped
1 clove of garlic, crushed
150ml/¼ pint dry white wine
2 × 15ml spoons/2 tablespoons finely chopped parsley
100g/4 oz stelline (small pasta stars)

Split the lobster lengthways. Pull out the intestinal tract and clear out the head cavity. Remove the gills. Remove the meat carefully from the shell, and dice it.

Put the shell into a pan with the water and salt and pepper to taste. Bring to the boil, then reduce the heat and simmer for 20 minutes. Strain and reserve the lobster stock.

Melt the butter in a large pan and gently fry the onion for 4 minutes. Add the chopped tomatoes and garlic, and fry gently for a further 2 minutes. Add the strained lobster stock, the white wine and parsley, and simmer for 10 minutes. Add the diced lobster meat and the stelline, and simmer for 2 minutes until the pasta is just tender. Serve the soup piping hot.

Note A fishmonger may well prepare the lobster, if necessary.

Zuppa di Gamberi
SHRIMP AND BASIL SOUP

2 × 15ml spoons/2 tablespoons olive oil
25g/1 oz butter
2 medium carrots, chopped
3 sticks celery, cut into strips
1 × 15ml spoon/1 tablespoon chopped fresh basil
2 × 15ml spoons/2 tablespoons chopped parsley
1 medium onion, finely chopped
salt, freshly ground black pepper
225g/8 oz peeled shrimps **or** prawns
1.2 litres/2 pints Brodo di Pollo
(chicken stock, page 19)
150ml/¼ pint Marsala
75g/3 oz farfalle (pasta bows)
4 × 15ml spoons/4 tablespoons double cream

GARNISH (optional)
unpeeled shrimps

Heat the oil and butter in a large pan. Add the carrots, celery, basil, parsley and onion, and fry gently for 5 minutes. Season to taste, then add the shrimps and chicken stock. Bring to the boil, then reduce the heat and simmer for 20 minutes. Add the Marsala and bring back to the boil. Add the farfalle and simmer gently for 5–6 minutes until the pasta is tender. Stir in the cream, adjust seasoning to taste, and heat through. Serve the hot soup in warmed soup bowls, garnishing each portion with one or two unpeeled shrimps, if liked.

ZUPPA DI CASTAGNE CON LUMACHINE
CHESTNUT SOUP WITH SMALL PASTA SNAILS

225g/8 oz chestnuts
50g/2 oz butter
1 large onion, finely chopped
2 medium carrots, finely chopped
1 celery stalk, finely chopped
salt, freshly ground black pepper
900ml/1½ pints Brodo di Manzo (beef stock, page 20)
300ml/½ pint dry white wine
3 × 15ml spoons/3 tablespoons medium sherry
75g/3 oz lumachine (small pasta snails)

Score the shell of each chestnut. Put them on to a baking sheet and bake in a warm oven, 160°C/325°F/Gas 3, for 15 minutes. Peel off the shells and skins from the chestnuts while they are still warm.

Melt the butter in a large pan and cook the onion, carrots and celery until lightly golden. Add the chestnuts, salt and pepper to taste, the stock and the wine. Bring to the boil, then reduce the heat and simmer until the chestnuts are quite tender. Blend the soup in a liquidizer or food processor, or sieve it until smooth. Return to a clean pan, add the sherry and heat through gently.

Meanwhile, cook the lumachine in a pan of boiling salted water until just tender. Drain thoroughly and add to the soup. Serve in warmed soup bowls.

ZUPPA DI CAPELLI D'ANGELO
VERMICELLI AND COURGETTE SOUP

25g/1 oz butter
2 × 15ml spoons/2 tablespoons olive oil
1 small onion, finely chopped
225g/8 oz courgettes, cut into 5mm/¼ inch thick slices
salt, freshly ground black pepper
1 litre/1¾ pints Brodo di Pollo
(chicken stock, page 19)
150ml/¼ pint dry white wine
2 eggs
1 × 15ml spoon/1 tablespoon chopped parsley
1 × 15ml spoon/1 tablespoon chopped fresh basil
25g/1 oz Parmesan cheese, grated
75g/3 oz capelli d'angelo (very fine vermicelli)

Heat the butter and oil in a large pan. Add the onion and fry gently for 2–3 minutes. Add the courgettes and fry for a further 2–3 minutes. Season to taste. Add the stock and wine and bring to the boil, then reduce the heat and simmer for 15 minutes.

Beat the eggs with the parsley, basil and Parmesan cheese. Beat a little of the hot soup liquid into the egg mixture, and then return the egg mixture to the remaining soup. Bring the soup back just to the boil, then add the vermicelli. Reduce the heat and simmer for 2 minutes. Serve the soup in warmed soup bowls.

Zuppa alla Paesana
PEASANT-STYLE LENTIL SOUP

350g/12 oz dried lentils
salt, freshly ground black pepper
1 × 15ml spoon/1 tablespoon olive oil
25g/1 oz butter
4 sticks celery, sliced
1 small head of fennel, shredded
1 large clove of garlic, crushed
2 × 15ml spoons/2 tablespoons chopped parsley
450g/1 lb ripe Mediterranean tomatoes, skinned,
de-seeded and roughly chopped
1.2 litres/2 pints Brodo di Manzo (beef stock, page 20)
50g/2 oz wholewheat pasta rings
2 × 15ml spoons/2 tablespoons Parmesan cheese, grated

GARNISH
4 feathery sprigs fennel

Soak the lentils in cold water for 6 hours or overnight, then drain them and put into a pan. Add enough fresh cold water just to cover, and 1 × 5ml spoon/1 teaspoon salt. Cover, bring to the boil and simmer for about 50 minutes – 1 hour until the lentils are just tender.

Meanwhile, heat the oil and butter in a large pan. Add the celery and fennel and fry gently for 5 minutes. Add the garlic, parsley, tomatoes and beef stock. Bring to the boil, then reduce the heat and simmer for 15 minutes. Drain the cooked lentils and add to the soup.

Cook the pasta rings in a pan of boiling salted water until just tender. Drain thoroughly and add to the soup. Season to taste with salt and pepper, and heat through. Serve the soup in warmed soup bowls. Sprinkle each portion with a little grated Parmesan cheese and garnish with a sprig of fennel.

Zuppa di Ceci
CHICK-PEA AND PASTA SOUP

350g/12 oz dried chick-peas
salt, freshly ground black pepper
2 sprigs fresh rosemary
1 bay leaf
2 × 15ml spoons/2 tablespoons olive oil
6 anchovy fillets, drained and chopped
1 large clove of garlic, crushed
6 ripe Mediterranean tomatoes,
skinned, de-seeded and roughly chopped
1.2 litres/2 pints Brodo di Pollo
(chicken stock, page 19)
75g/3 oz lumachine (small pasta snails)

Soak the chick-peas in plenty of cold water for 6 hours or overnight. Drain them, put into a pan, and add sufficient fresh cold water just to cover them. Add 1 × 5ml spoon/1 teaspoon salt, the rosemary and bay leaf. Bring to the boil, then reduce the heat and simmer for about 45 minutes until the chick-peas are tender. Remove the rosemary and bay leaf. Blend the chick-peas and their cooking liquid in a liquidizer or food processor, or sieve until smooth.

Heat the oil in a large pan, add the anchovy fillets and garlic and fry gently for 1 minute. Add the tomatoes and chicken stock and simmer for 10 minutes, then stir in the puréed chick-peas and simmer for 5 minutes.

Meanwhile, cook the lumachine in a pan of boiling salted water until just tender. Drain thoroughly and add to the hot soup. (If necessary, thin the soup down with a little extra hot stock). Season to taste with salt and pepper, and serve in warmed soup bowls.

Pasta e Fagioli (page 21), Zuppa alla Paesana **and** *Zuppa di Gamberi (page 24)*

ZUPPA VERDE CON SPAGHETTINI
WATERCRESS AND SPAGHETTINI SOUP

2 bunches watercress, trimmed and chopped
2 onions, sliced
1.2 litres/2 pints Brodo di Pollo
(chicken stock, page 19)
salt, freshly ground black pepper
75g/3 oz spaghettini, broken into 5cm/2 inch lengths

GARNISH
2 hard-boiled eggs, finely chopped

Put the watercress into a pan with the onions, stock and salt and pepper to taste. Bring to the boil, then reduce the heat and simmer for 15 minutes. Add the spaghettini and simmer for a further 4 minutes until the pasta is tender. Serve in warmed soup bowls, topped with chopped hard-boiled egg.

ZUPPA DI VERDURE CON FARFALLETTE
LEEK AND PASTA SOUP

Serves 4–6

25g/1 oz butter
1 onion, finely chopped
1kg/2¼ lb leeks, sliced
1 large potato, peeled and sliced
1 litre/1¾ pints Brodo di Pollo
(chicken stock, page 19)
salt, freshly ground black pepper
175g/6 oz farfallette (small pasta bows)

Melt the butter in a large pan and gently fry the onion for 5 minutes. Add the leeks and potato and cook for 5 minutes. Add the stock and bring to the boil. Season to taste, then cover, reduce the heat and simmer until the leeks are cooked. Blend the soup in a liquidizer or food processor, or sieve until smooth, then return to the pan. Add the farfallette and simmer for 2–3 minutes until the pasta is tender. Serve the soup in warmed soup bowls.

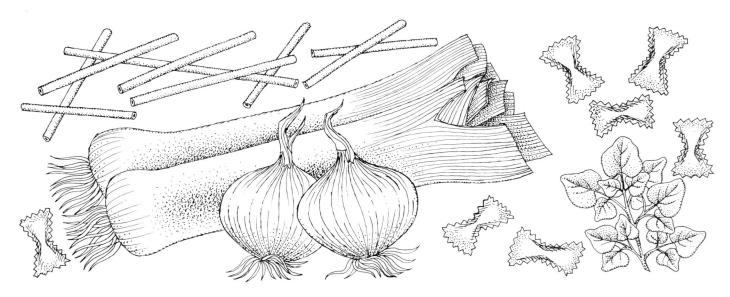

PASTA AS A MAIN COURSE

If you mention pasta to many people, they will think immediately of Spaghetti Bolognese. This is not necessarily an insult to pasta, merely a simple fact that they are unaware as to the permutations that pasta has to offer as a main meal. It is such a versatile food that it can be served as a starter as in Italy, in which case the recipes which follow will serve six rather than four people. The richer, more elaborate, pasta recipes should, however, be kept as main courses. Fish, meat, poultry and eggs all blend particularly well with pasta, offering a great repertoire of main meal dishes, some extremely simple and others a little more complicated.

A simple way of serving pasta is to toss the cooked, drained pasta very quickly in melted butter or a good quality olive oil, adding salt and freshly ground black pepper and grated nutmeg or chopped fresh herbs, if liked. Stir briefly over gentle heat, and spoon into warmed bowls. Serve immediately with grated Parmesan cheese.

The pasta and sauces are best prepared in a solid-based pan so that there is no danger of the pasta or other ingredients sticking to the pan.

Vegetables can be served as an accompaniment to a pasta main dish, but a really good tossed salad is more complimentary. Vary the salad ingredients according to the main course recipe. Crisp lettuce always makes a good base. For a fish pasta, add finely shredded raw fennel; for game or poultry, try using a few nuts and perhaps also some peeled orange segments; for meat-based pasta dishes, add a little thinly sliced raw onion, slivers of radish and chopped pepper, and for pasta dishes using egg, add black olives, chopped anchovy fillets or capers to the salad. Fresh herbs, when available, lift a salad into the super class.

SPAGHETTI ALLA BOLOGNESE
SPAGHETTI WITH MEAT SAUCE

75g/3 oz butter
2 × 15ml spoons/2 tablespoons olive oil
100g/4 oz smoked **or** cured Italian ham, chopped
1 medium onion, finely chopped
2 stalks celery, finely chopped
225g/8 oz minced beef
175g/6 oz chicken livers, chopped
100g/4 oz button mushrooms, chopped
2 × 15ml spoons/2 tablespoons concentrated tomato purée
150ml/$\frac{1}{4}$ pint Brodo di Manzo (beef stock, page 20)
150ml/$\frac{1}{4}$ pint red wine
2 × 15ml spoons/2 tablespoons Marsala
1 large clove of garlic, crushed
salt, freshly ground black pepper
2 × 15ml spoons/2 tablespoons double cream
350g/12 oz spaghetti

GARNISH
2 × 15ml spoons/2 tablespoons chopped parsley

Heat 50g/2 oz butter and 1 × 15ml spoon/1 tablespoon olive oil in a pan. Add the chopped ham and onion and fry gently for 3 minutes. Add the chopped celery, minced beef and chicken livers and stir over heat until evenly browned. Add the remaining ingredients, apart from the leftover butter and oil and the spaghetti. Bring to the boil, then reduce the heat and simmer the sauce for 30 minutes.

Meanwhile, cook the spaghetti in a large pan of steadily boiling water until *al dente* with the remaining oil and 1 × 5ml spoon/1 teaspoon salt. Drain thoroughly, then melt the remaining butter and toss the spaghetti in it. Pile on to a hot serving dish and spoon the hot Bolognese sauce over the top. Sprinkle with chopped parsley, and serve with a bowl of grated Parmesan or Pecorino cheese.

Note The Bolognese sauce is also known as *Ragu*.

SPAGHETTI ALLA CARBONARA
SPAGHETTI WITH BACON AND EGG SAUCE

Serves 4–6

350g/12 oz spaghetti
4 × 15ml spoons/4 tablespoons olive oil
salt, freshly ground black pepper
1 medium onion, finely chopped
6 rashers bacon, rinds removed and chopped
6 × 15ml spoons/6 tablespoons dry white wine
Parmesan   4 eggs
75g/3 oz Pecorino cheese, grated *Fine*
1 large clove of garlic, crushed
1 × 15ml spoon/1 tablespoon chopped fresh basil
cut down on basil

Cook the spaghetti in a large pan of steadily boiling water until *al dente* with 1 × 15ml spoon/1 tablespoon olive oil and 1 × 5ml spoon/1 teaspoon salt.

Meanwhile, heat the remaining olive oil in a pan, add the onion and fry gently for 4 minutes. Add the chopped bacon and fry for a minute or two. Add the white wine, and boil briskly until nearly all the liquid has evaporated. Beat the eggs with the Pecorino cheese, garlic, basil and salt and pepper to taste.

Drain the cooked spaghetti thoroughly and quickly stir in the beaten egg mixture and the bacon so that the heat from the pasta lightly cooks the egg. Serve immediately.

All ing. ready + fry onion, bacon + boil wine before pasta in pot.

CANNELLONI CON SALAME
SALAMI STUFFED CANNELLONI

175g/6 oz fresh lasagne **or** dry packeted lasagne
2 × 15ml spoons/2 tablespoons olive oil
salt, freshly ground black pepper
1 large onion, chopped
100g/4 oz cup mushrooms, sliced
225g/8 oz salami, diced
450g/1 lb Mediterranean tomatoes, skinned,
de-seeded and chopped
1 × 15ml spoon/1 tablespoon cornflour
600ml/1 pint Salsa Beschiamella
(savoury white sauce, page 64)
100g/4 oz Pecorino cheese, grated

GARNISH
sprigs parsley

If using dried lasagne, pre-cook it in a pan of steadily boiling water for about 6 minutes with 1 × 15ml spoon/1 tablespoon olive oil and 1 × 5ml spoon/1 teaspoon salt. Use fresh lasagne as it is.

Meanwhile, heat the remaining oil in a pan and cook the onion until soft. Add the mushrooms and soften them, then add the salami and tomatoes. Mix together well. Blend the corn-flour with a little water to form a smooth paste, then add to the salami mixture. Simmer for 2 minutes until the mixture has thickened. Season well.

Drain the dried lasagne thoroughly, cut the sheets in half (fresh or dried) and place the salami mixture in the centre. Roll them up and place either in four greased individual ovenproof dishes (three to a dish) or in one large ovenproof dish.

Mix the sauce with half the grated cheese, then pour it over the cannelloni and sprinkle with the remaining cheese. Cook in a fairly hot oven, 190°C/375°F/Gas 5, until golden-brown. Garnish with sprigs of parsley and serve immediately.

Serve with a crisp salad.

Cannelloni con Salame

SPAGHETTINI TETRAZZINI
BAKED SPAGHETTINI WITH BACON AND CHICKEN

175g/6 oz spaghettini
1 × 15ml spoon/1 tablespoon olive oil
salt, freshly ground black pepper
175g/6 oz streaky bacon, rinds removed and chopped
2 red peppers, de-seeded and chopped
225g/8 oz cooked chicken, chopped
40g/1½ oz butter
40g/1½ oz flour
150ml/¼ pint milk
450ml/¾ pint Brodo di Pollo (chicken stock, page 19)
75g/3 oz Bel Paese cheese, grated
½ × 2.5ml spoon/¼ teaspoon grated nutmeg
2 × 15ml spoons/2 tablespoons sherry
1 egg yolk
25g/1 oz flaked almonds

Cook the spaghettini in a large pan of steadily boiling water until *al dente* with the oil and 1 × 5ml spoon/1 teaspoon salt.

Meanwhile, fry the bacon and peppers gently in a large pan until the bacon is crisp but not brown. Add the chicken and cook for a further 5 minutes. Drain the pasta thoroughly and gently stir into the mixture, then remove from the heat.

Melt the butter in a clean pan, add the flour, then slowly add the milk and stock. Bring to the boil, stirring constantly, and leave the sauce to thicken. Add the cheese, then season to taste with salt and pepper and add the nutmeg and sherry. Off the heat, stir in the egg yolk.

Place the chicken mixture in an ovenproof dish, coat with the sauce and sprinkle with the flaked almonds. Cook in a fairly hot oven, 190°C/375°F/Gas 5, for about 25 minutes until bubbling and golden. Serve immediately.

MACCHERONI CON SALAME E VERDURE
MACARONI WITH SALAMI AND VEGETABLES

4 × 15ml spoons/4 tablespoons olive oil
1 medium onion, finely chopped
1 large clove of garlic, crushed
450g/1 lb Mediterranean tomatoes,
skinned, de-seeded and chopped
1 red pepper, de-seeded and cut into strips
225g/8 oz courgettes, thinly sliced
175g/6 oz Italian salami, cubed
salt, freshly ground black pepper
350g/12 oz elbow maccheroni
40g/1½ oz butter, melted

Heat 3 × 15ml spoons/3 tablespoons olive oil in a pan. Add the onion and fry gently for 3 minutes. Add the garlic and chopped tomatoes and bring to the boil. Reduce the heat and simmer steadily until the tomatoes are really soft and pulpy. Add the pepper, courgettes, salami and salt and pepper to taste, and simmer until the vegetables are just tender.

Meanwhile, cook the maccheroni in a large pan of steadily boiling water until *al dente* with the remaining oil and 1 × 5ml spoon/1 teaspoon salt. Drain thoroughly and toss in the melted butter. Gently stir in the prepared hot vegetable and salami sauce. Serve immediately.

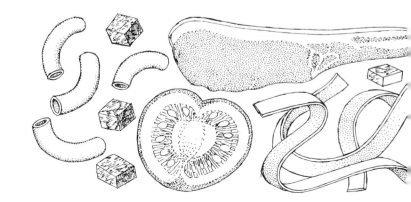

TAGLIATELLE VERDE AMATRICIANA
TAGLIATELLE WITH BACON AND PARMESAN SAUCE

50g/2 oz butter
1 medium onion, thinly sliced
150ml/¼ pint dry white wine
225g/8 oz lean bacon, rinds removed and chopped
1 × 15ml spoon/1 tablespoon chopped basil
1 × 15ml spoon/1 tablespoon chopped parsley
450g/1 lb Mediterranean tomatoes,
skinned, de-seeded and chopped
salt, freshly ground black pepper
350g/12 oz tagliatelle verde
1 × 15ml spoon/1 tablespoon olive oil
75g/3 oz Parmesan cheese, grated

Melt the butter in a pan and cook the onion until golden. Add the wine, bacon, herbs, tomatoes and salt and pepper to taste. Simmer gently for 15 minutes, stirring occasionally.

Meanwhile, cook the tagliatelle in a large pan of steadily boiling water until *al dente* with the oil and 1 × 5ml spoon/ 1 teaspoon salt. Drain thoroughly and pile on to a hot serving dish. Spoon the hot sauce over the top to coat thoroughly. Sprinkle generously with Parmesan cheese, toss and serve immediately.

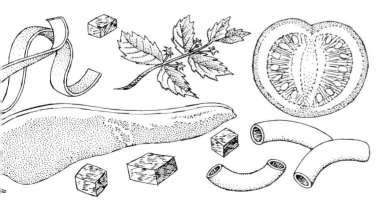

CARCIOFFI CON PASTA
PASTA STUFFED ARTICHOKES

Serves 6

6 globe artichokes
1 lemon
salt, freshly ground black pepper
25g/1 oz butter
1 medium onion, finely chopped
300ml/½ pint Salsa Besciamella
(savoury white sauce, page 64)
3 eggs, separated
75g/3 oz Parmesan cheese, grated
100g/4 oz lean Italian ham, finely chopped
50g/2 oz tagliatelle verde, broken into pieces

Cut a 2.5cm/1 inch slice from the top of each artichoke. Trim off the tip of each leaf with kitchen scissors. Halve the lemon and rub all the cut surfaces of the artichokes with half the lemon. Bring a large pan of water to the boil. Add 1 × 5ml spoon/1 teaspoon salt and the juice from the remaining half lemon to the pan. Add the prepared globe artichokes, cover the pan and simmer steadily for about 25 minutes until the artichokes are tender. Pull on one of the lower leaves and if it comes away readily the artichoke is ready. Drain the cooked artichokes, cut surfaces downwards, on absorbent kitchen paper.

Melt the butter in a pan and gently fry the chopped onion for 3 minutes. Stir in the sauce, egg yolks, two-thirds of the Parmesan cheese, salt and pepper to taste, and the chopped ham.

Remove the centre leaves from each artichoke (these can be used in soup) and the centre 'hairy choke'. Stand the hollowed artichoke upright in a greased baking dish.

Cook the tagliatelle in boiling salted water for about 3–4 minutes until tender, then drain thoroughly. Meanwhile, whisk the egg whites until stiff but not dry.

Fold the egg whites and cooked tagliatelle into the sauce mixture lightly but thoroughly. Spoon carefully into the centre of each hollowed artichoke, and sprinkle with the remaining grated Parmesan cheese. Cook in a fairly hot oven, 190°C/375°F/Gas 5, for about 40–50 minutes until the centres are risen and golden. Serve immediately before the centres of the artichokes have a chance to collapse.

LASAGNE DI CARNE MISTO
TURKEY AND ITALIAN HAM LASAGNE

Serves 4–6

50g/2 oz butter
1 medium onion, finely chopped
25g/1 oz flour
300ml/½ pint Brodo di Pollo (chicken stock, page 19)
150ml/¼ pint milk
a pinch of grated nutmeg
salt, freshly ground black pepper
100g/4 oz Italian ham, finely chopped
225g/8 oz cooked turkey, finely chopped
175g/6 oz fresh lasagne verde **or**
dry packeted lasagne (see **Note**)
100g/4 oz button mushrooms, sliced
juice of 1 lemon
200ml/⅓ pint soured cream
1 egg
75g/3 oz Pecorino cheese, grated

Melt half the butter in a pan and cook the onion until soft. Stir in the flour and cook for 1 minute. Gradually add the stock and milk, and bring to the boil, stirring constantly, until the sauce has thickened. Add the nutmeg, salt and pepper to taste, the ham and the chopped turkey.

Spread one-third of the sauce over the base of a greased rectangular glass casserole; arrange one-third of the lasagne on top, and repeat until the sauce and lasagne are used. Finish with a layer of lasagne.

Melt the remaining butter in a clean pan and gently cook the mushrooms with the lemon juice. Arrange them on top of the lasagne. Beat the soured cream with the egg and spoon this evenly over the mushrooms. Sprinkle with the grated cheese. Cook in a fairly hot oven, 190°C/375°F/Gas 5, for 30–35 minutes until bubbling and golden. Serve immediately.

Note If using dry packeted lasagne, use only the variety which requires no previous cooking.

LASAGNE AL FORNO
BAKED MEAT LASAGNE

Serves 4–6

3 × 15ml spoons/3 tablespoons olive oil
50g/2 oz Italian ham, chopped
1 medium onion, finely chopped
450g/1 lb minced lean beef
1 large clove of garlic, crushed
3 × 15ml spoons/3 tablespoons concentrated
tomato purée
600ml/1 pint Brodo di Pollo (chicken stock, page 19)
salt, freshly ground black pepper
175g/6 oz fresh lasagne **or**
dry packeted lasagne (see **Note**)
225g/8 oz Bel Paese **or** Fontina cheese,
rinds removed and thinly sliced
300ml/½ pint Salsa Besciamella
(savoury white sauce, page 64)
3 × 15ml spoons/3 tablespoons Parmesan cheese, grated

Heat the oil in a large pan. Add the chopped ham and cook for 1–2 minutes to extract the fat. Add the chopped onion and fry gently for 4 minutes. Add the minced beef and cook until evenly browned. Add the garlic, tomato purée, stock and salt and pepper to taste. Cover, bring to the boil, then reduce the heat and simmer gently for 45 minutes.

Spread one-third of the meat sauce over the base of a greased rectangular gratin dish; arrange one-third of the lasagne on top, and follow with one-third of the Bel Paese or Fontina cheese. Repeat with two more layers of meat sauce, lasagne and sliced cheese. Spoon the prepared sauce evenly over the top, then sprinkle with the grated Parmesan cheese. Cook in a fairly hot oven, 190°C/375°F/Gas 5, for about 45 minutes until bubbling and golden. Serve immediately.

Note If using dry packeted lasagne, use only the variety which requires no previous cooking.

Lasagne di Carne Misto

34

FUSILLI ALLA CARUSO
SPAGHETTI WITH LIVER AND MUSHROOM SAUCE

350g/12 oz fusilli (twisted spaghetti)
4 × 15ml spoons/4 tablespoons olive oil
salt, freshly ground black pepper
1 medium onion, finely chopped
1 clove of garlic, crushed
175g/6 oz calf's liver, chopped
100g/4 oz button mushrooms, sliced
350g/12 oz Mediterranean tomatoes,
skinned and sieved
1 × 5ml spoon/1 teaspoon chopped parsley

Cook the fusilli in a large pan of steadily boiling water until *al dente* with 1 × 15ml spoon/1 tablespoon oil and 1 × 5ml spoon/ 1 teaspoon salt.

Meanwhile, heat the remaining oil in a pan and cook the onion until soft, then add the crushed garlic. Add the liver and cook gently for 2 minutes, then add the mushrooms, tomatoes and parsley. Simmer for 4–5 minutes and season to taste.

Drain the cooked pasta thoroughly and gently stir in the prepared hot sauce. Serve immediately.

TAGLIATELLE CON SALSA DI PROSCIUTTO
TAGLIATELLE WITH HAM AND MUSHROOM SAUCE

350g/12 oz tagliatelle verde
1 × 15ml spoon/1 tablespoon olive oil
salt, freshly ground black pepper
25g/1 oz butter
225g/8 oz Italian ham, chopped
100g/4 oz button mushrooms, sliced
300ml/½ pint Salsa Beschiamella
(savoury white sauce, page 64)
4 × 15ml spoons/4 tablespoons double cream

Cook the tagliatelle in a large pan of steadily boiling water until *al dente* with the oil and 1 × 5ml spoon/1 teaspoon salt.

Meanwhile, melt the butter in a pan and cook the chopped ham for 2 minutes. Remove from the pan and cook the mushrooms in the remaining fat. Transfer the ham and mushrooms to a clean pan and mix together with the sauce and salt and pepper to taste. Stir in the cream and heat through.

Drain the pasta thoroughly and arrange around the outside of a dish. Pour the sauce into the centre and serve immediately.

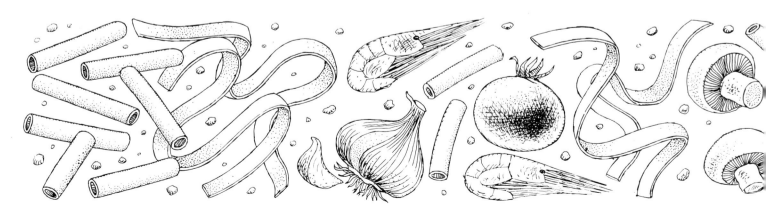

PASTA E POLLO
PASTA AND CHICKEN SCALLOPS

350g/12 oz ditali (thimble macaroni)
4 × 15ml spoons/4 tablespoons olive oil
salt, freshly ground black pepper
1 large onion, finely chopped
4 rashers bacon, rinds removed and chopped
225g/8 oz button mushrooms, chopped **or** sliced
300ml/½ pint double cream
225g/8 oz cooked chicken, chopped
4 × 15ml spoons/4 tablespoons fresh breadcrumbs
75g/3 oz Bel Paese **or** Fontina cheese, grated

GARNISH
sprigs parsley

Cook the pasta in a large pan of steadily boiling water until *al dente* with 1 × 15ml spoon/1 tablespoon olive oil and 1 × 5ml spoon/1 teaspoon salt.

Meanwhile, heat the remaining oil in a pan and cook the onion for 2 minutes. Add the bacon and mushrooms and cook for a further 3–4 minutes. Drain the pasta thoroughly and stir into the mixture with the cream and chopped chicken. Season to taste with salt and pepper, then spoon into four greased scallop shells or one large gratin dish. Sprinkle with the breadcrumbs and the grated cheese and brown under a moderate grill. Garnish with parsley sprigs.

MACCHERONI AL FORNO
MACARONI AND PRAWN LAYER BAKE

350g/12 oz maccheroni
1 × 15ml spoon/1 tablespoon olive oil
salt, freshly ground black pepper
50g/2 oz butter
175g/6 oz button mushrooms, finely sliced
175g/6 oz shelled prawns
600ml/1 pint Salsa Beschiamella
(savoury white sauce, page 64)
50g/2 oz Parmesan cheese, grated

GARNISH
unpeeled prawns

Cook the maccheroni in a large pan of steadily boiling water until *al dente* with the oil and 1 × 5ml spoon/1 teaspoon salt.

Meanwhile, melt the butter in a pan and cook the mushrooms until soft. Add the prawns off heat, then mix them with the sauce, and season to taste with salt and pepper.

Drain the pasta thoroughly, then fill a buttered ovenproof dish with alternate layers of pasta and prawn and mushroom sauce, starting with pasta and finishing with the sauce. Sprinkle with the Parmesan cheese and cook in a fairly hot oven, 190°C/375°F/Gas 5, for 20–25 minutes until bubbling. Garnish with whole prawns and serve immediately.

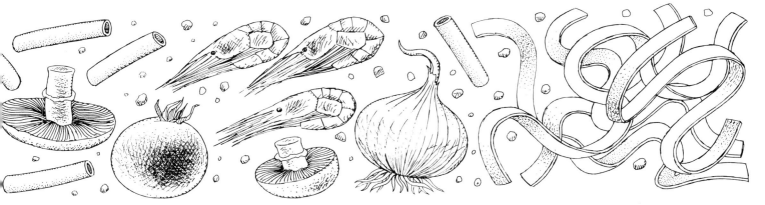

LASAGNE ALLA PESCE
FISH LASAGNE

Serves 4–6

350g/12 oz cooked white fish, flaked
200g/7 oz canned tuna fish in brine,
drained and coarsely flaked
600ml/1 pint Sugo di Pomodoro e Panna
(tomato and cream sauce, page 72)
2 × 15ml spoons/2 tablespoons chopped parsley
4 anchovy fillets, drained and chopped
salt, freshly ground black pepper
4 Mediterranean tomatoes, skinned, de-seeded
and chopped
50g/2 oz plump black olives, pitted and chopped
2 × 5ml spoons/2 teaspoons capers
175g/6 oz fresh lasagne **or** dry packeted lasagne
(see **Note**)
225g/8 oz Mozzarella cheese, thinly sliced
2 × 15ml spoons/2 tablespoons fine breadcrumbs
2 × 15ml spoons/2 tablespoons olive oil

Mix the white fish with the tuna, tomato and cream sauce, parsley, anchovy fillets, salt and pepper to taste, chopped tomatoes, olives and capers. Spread one-third of the mixture over the base of a greased rectangular gratin dish; arrange one-third of the lasagne on top, and follow with one-third of the Mozzarella cheese. Repeat with two more layers of fish and sauce mixture, lasagne and sliced cheese. Sprinkle the top with the breadcrumbs and olive oil. Cook in a fairly hot oven, 190°C/375°F/Gas 5, for about 45 minutes until bubbling and golden. Serve immediately.

Note   If using dry packeted lasagne, use only the variety which requires no previous cooking.

Variation
Use flaked canned or fresh cooked salmon in place of the canned tuna.

PAPPARDELLE ALLA PUTTANESCA
NOODLES WITH TOMATO AND ANCHOVY SAUCE

2 × 15ml spoons/2 tablespoons olive oil
3 cloves garlic, chopped
675g/1½ lb Mediterranean tomatoes
skinned, de-seeded and chopped
1 × 15ml spoon/1 tablespoon fresh oregano, chopped
6 anchovy fillets, drained and chopped
12 black olives
1 × 15ml spoon/1 tablespoon capers
salt, freshly ground black pepper
350g/12 oz pappardelle (wide ribbon noodles)

GARNISH
chopped parsley

Heat 1 × 15ml spoon/1 tablespoon olive oil in a pan and cook the garlic until golden. Add the chopped tomatoes, the oregano, anchovies, olives and capers. Season to taste with salt and pepper, and simmer for about 15 minutes, stirring frequently.

Meanwhile, cook the pappardelle in a large pan of steadily boiling water until *al dente* with the remaining oil and 1 × 5ml spoon/1 teaspoon salt. Drain thoroughly, then pile on to a hot serving dish and spoon the sauce over the top. Toss carefully, then sprinkle with chopped parsley and freshly ground pepper. Serve immediately.

Pappardelle alla Puttanesca

Maccheroni con Gamberi
MACARONI WITH PRAWNS

Serves 4–6

175g/6 oz elbow maccheroni
1 × 15ml spoon/1 tablespoon olive oil
salt, freshly ground black pepper
75g/3 oz shelled prawns
2 eggs, beaten
3 × 15ml spoons/3 tablespoons soured cream
5 × 15ml spoons/5 tablespoons breadcrumbs
25g/1 oz butter

Cook the pasta in a large pan of steadily boiling water until *al dente* with the oil and 1 × 5ml spoon/1 teaspoon salt. Drain thoroughly, then mix together with the prawns, eggs and soured cream. Season to taste with salt and pepper. Transfer to a greased gratin dish, top with the breadcrumbs and dot with small knobs of butter. Cook in a fairly hot oven, 190°C/375°F/Gas 5, for 25 minutes until bubbling. Serve immediately.

Tagliatelle al Tonno
TAGLIATELLE WITH TUNA AND MUSHROOM SAUCE

350g/12 oz tagliatelle verde and plain tagliatelle
1 × 15ml spoon/1 tablespoon olive oil
salt, freshly ground black pepper
200g/7 oz canned tuna fish in oil
1 medium onion, chopped
100g/4 oz button mushrooms, sliced
150ml/¼ pint double cream

Cook the tagliatelle in a large pan of steadily boiling water until *al dente* with the oil and 1 × 5ml spoon/1 teaspoon salt.

Meanwhile, drain the oil from the tuna into a large pan, and cook the chopped onion until soft. Add the sliced mushrooms and cook until soft, then season to taste with salt and pepper.

Drain the pasta thoroughly and add to the pan. Pour in the cream and mix together over low heat. Adjust seasoning to taste and serve immediately.

PASTA AL PESCATORE
FISHERMAN'S PASTA

225g/8 oz elbow maccheroni
1 × 15ml spoon/1 tablespoon olive oil
salt, freshly ground black pepper
25g/1 oz butter
200ml/⅓ pint single cream
grated rind of ½ lemon
2 × 15ml spoons/2 tablespoons chopped parsley
200g/7 oz canned tuna fish, drained and flaked
100g/4 oz peeled prawns

GARNISH
unpeeled prawns
sprigs parsley

Cook the pasta in a large pan of steadily boiling water until *al dente* with the oil and 1 × 5ml spoon/1 teaspoon salt.

Meanwhile, melt the butter in a pan and stir in the cream, lemon rind, chopped parsley, flaked tuna and peeled prawns.

Drain the pasta thoroughly and add to the pan. Season to taste with salt and pepper, and heat through gently. Garnish with a few unpeeled prawns and parsley sprigs. Serve immediately.

FETTUCINE ALLA GORGONZOLA
FETTUCINE WITH GORGONZOLA SAUCE

350g/12 oz fettucine
2 × 15ml spoons/2 tablespoons olive oil
salt, freshly ground black pepper
4 rashers bacon, rinds removed and chopped
1 large clove of garlic, crushed
300ml/½ pint single cream
175g/6 oz Gorgonzola, finely crumbled
1 × 15ml spoon/1 tablespoon chopped fresh sage

Cook the fettucine in a large pan of steadily boiling water until *al dente* with 1 × 15ml spoon/1 tablespoon olive oil and 1 × 5ml spoon/1 teaspoon salt.

Meanwhile, heat the remaining oil in a pan and fry the chopped bacon for 3–4 minutes. Add the garlic, cream, crumbled Gorgonzola, sage and salt and pepper to taste, and heat through.

Drain the cooked fettucine thoroughly and gently stir in the prepared hot sauce. Serve immediately.

PASTA PASTICCIATA
PASTA PIE

Serves 6

175g/6 oz vermicelli
salt, freshly ground black pepper
3 × 15ml spoons/3 tablespoons olive oil
5 eggs, beaten
freshly grated nutmeg
2 × 15ml spoons/2 tablespoons finely chopped parsley
1 medium onion, thinly sliced
350g/12 oz cold cooked spinach, chopped
100g/4 oz full fat cream cheese, softened
150ml/¼ pint single cream
1 × 15ml spoon/1 tablespoon chopped fresh basil
2 × 15ml spoons/2 tablespoons Pecorino cheese, grated

Cook the vermicelli in boiling salted water for 2 minutes, then drain thoroughly. Mix with salt and pepper to taste, 1 × 15ml spoon/1 tablespoon of the olive oil, two beaten eggs, a little freshly grated nutmeg and the chopped parsley. Press the noodle mixture over the base and up the sides of a greased 22.5cm/9 inch flan dish. Cover the rim of the pasta with foil and cook in a fairly hot oven, 190°C/375°F/Gas 5, for 10 minutes until set.

Meanwhile, heat the remaining oil in a pan and gently fry the sliced onion for 5 minutes. Mix with the spinach and salt, pepper and nutmeg to taste. Beat the cream cheese with the cream and remaining eggs until smooth.

Mix together the spinach and cream cheese mixtures, and add the chopped basil. Spread the filling evenly into the pasta shell and sprinkle with the Pecorino cheese. Bake for a further 25–30 minutes until the filling is set. Serve warm, cut into wedges.

SPAGHETTI CON FORMAGGIO E NOCE
SPAGHETTI WITH RICOTTA AND ALMONDS

100g/4 oz ground almonds
100g/4 oz ricotta
a pinch of ground cinnamon
a pinch of grated nutmeg
150ml/¼ pint single cream
4 × 15ml spoons/4 tablespoons olive oil
25g/1 oz Parmesan cheese, grated
salt, freshly ground black pepper
350g/12 oz spaghetti
50g/2 oz butter, melted
1 × 15ml spoon/1 tablespoon chopped parsley

GARNISH
flaked toasted almonds

Mix together the ground almonds with the ricotta, cinnamon, nutmeg, cream and 3 × 15ml spoons/3 tablespoons of the oil to make a thick paste. Add the Parmesan cheese and salt, and mix well.

Cook the spaghetti in a large pan of steadily boiling water until *al dente* with the remaining oil and 1 × 5ml spoon/1 teaspoon salt. Drain thoroughly, reserving 150ml/¼ pint of the water. Toss the spaghetti in the butter and chopped parsley and pile on to a warm serving dish.

Mix together the reserved water and the ricotta sauce and pour this over the spaghetti. Garnish with a few flaked toasted almonds and serve immediately.

Pasta Pasticciata

CONCHIGLIE AL FORMAGGIO
CHEESE AND PASTA SCALLOPS

Serves 4–6

350g/12 oz conchiglie (pasta shells)
1 × 15ml spoon/1 tablespoon olive oil
salt, freshly ground black pepper
6 rashers streaky bacon, rinds removed
3 hard-boiled eggs, chopped
600ml/1 pint Salsa Beschiamella
(savoury white sauce, page 64)
175g/6 oz Bel Paese cheese, grated

Cook the pasta in a large pan of steadily boiling water until *al dente* with the oil and 1 × 5ml spoon/1 teaspoon salt.

Meanwhile, grill the bacon until crisp, then cut into small pieces. Drain the pasta thoroughly, then mix with the bacon and chopped egg, reserving some of the bacon for the garnish.

Season the sauce to taste and add half the grated cheese. Arrange the pasta mixture in 4–6 large greased scallop shells, then top with the sauce and sprinkle with the remaining cheese and the reserved bacon pieces. Place under the grill for 5 minutes until browned. Serve immediately.

RAVIOLI CON BESCIAMELLA
RAVIOLI WITH WHITE SAUCE AND CHEESE

350g/12 oz fresh ravioli
1 × 15ml spoon/1 tablespoon olive oil
salt, freshly ground black pepper
40g/1½ oz butter, melted
300ml/½ pint Salsa Besciamella
(savoury white sauce, page 64)
2 × 15ml spoons/2 tablespoons single cream
100g/4 oz Mozzarella cheese, thinly sliced
2 × 15ml spoons/2 tablespoons Parmesan cheese, grated

Cook the ravioli in a large pan of steadily boiling water until *al dente* with the olive oil and 1 × 5ml spoon/1 teaspoon salt. Drain thoroughly and toss in the melted butter. Spoon the ravioli into a lightly greased shallow ovenproof dish. Mix the sauce with the cream and season to taste with salt and pepper. Spoon the sauce evenly over the ravioli. Lay the slices of Mozzarella on top and sprinkle with the grated Parmesan cheese. Cook in a fairly hot oven, 190°C/375°F/Gas 5, for 15 minutes until the sauce is lightly golden and bubbling. Serve immediately.

Fettucine all'Alfredo
FETTUCINE IN CREAM AND BUTTER SAUCE

350g/12 oz fettucine
1 × 15ml spoon/1 tablespoon olive oil
salt, freshly ground black pepper
50g/2 oz butter
1 clove of garlic, finely chopped
50g/2 oz Parmesan cheese, grated
freshly grated nutmeg
1 × 15ml spoon/1 tablespoon chopped fresh basil
200ml/⅓ pint double cream

Cook the fettucine in a large pan of steadily boiling water until
al dente with the oil and 1 × 5ml spoon/1 teaspoon salt.
  Meanwhile, melt the butter in a pan and cook the garlic for 1
minute.
  Drain the cooked fettucine thoroughly and gently stir into
the pan with the Parmesan cheese, salt, pepper and nutmeg to
taste, the basil and the cream. Stir over gentle heat for 1 minute
and serve immediately.

Cappelletti con la Panna
STUFFED PASTA HATS WITH
BUTTER AND CREAM

350g/12 oz cappelletti (stuffed pasta hats)
1 × 15ml spoon/1 tablespoon olive oil
salt, freshly ground black pepper
150ml/¼ pint double cream
50g/2 oz butter, melted
50g/2 oz Parmesan cheese, grated
1 × 15ml spoon/1 tablespoon chopped fresh coriander

Cook the cappelletti in a large pan of steadily boiling water until
al dente with the oil and 1 × 5ml spoon/1 teaspoon salt. Drain
thoroughly.
  Put the cream, melted butter, Parmesan cheese, coriander
and salt and pepper to taste into a clean pan. Add the cooked
pasta and stir over gentle heat for 1 minute. Serve immediately.

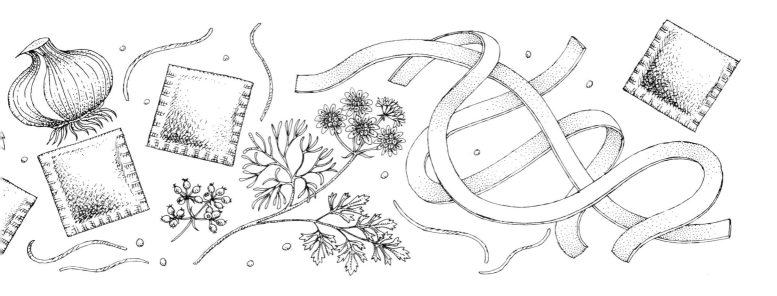

FETTUCINE CON SALSA DI NOCE
FETTUCINE WITH WALNUT SAUCE

350g/12 oz fettucine
1 × 15ml spoon/1 tablespoon olive oil
salt, freshly ground black pepper
50g/2 oz butter
75g/3 oz walnuts, finely chopped
1 large clove of garlic, crushed
3 × 15ml spoons/3 tablespoons Parmesan cheese, grated
4 × 15ml spoons/4 tablespoons Brodo di Pollo
(chicken stock, page 19)
2 × 15ml spoons/2 tablespoons soured cream

Cook the fettucine in a large pan of steadily boiling water until *al dente* with the oil and 1 × 5ml spoon/1 teaspoon salt.

Meanwhile, melt half the butter in a pan. Add the walnuts and garlic, and fry for 1 minute. Stir in the grated cheese and the chicken stock over heat.

Drain the cooked fettucine thoroughly, melt the remaining butter and toss the pasta in it, together with the soured cream. Season to taste with salt and pepper. Serve the pasta in individual bowls, topped with the hot walnut sauce.

Serve with a green salad.

FETTUCINE CON FAGIOLI
FETTUCINE WITH BEANS

300g/10 oz fettucine
5 × 15ml spoons/5 tablespoons olive oil
salt, freshly ground black pepper
3 cloves garlic, finely chopped
a generous pinch of chilli powder
425g/15 oz canned red kidney beans, drained
2 × 5ml spoons/2 teaspoons Pesto (page 65)
175g/6 oz Mozzarella cheese, diced

Cook the fettucine in a large pan of steadily boiling water until *al dente* with 1 × 15ml spoon/1 tablespoon olive oil and 1 × 5ml spoon/1 teaspoon salt.

Meanwhile, heat the remaining olive oil in a pan and fry the garlic gently without allowing it to colour. Stir in the chilli powder, red kidney beans, Pesto and salt and pepper to taste.

Drain the cooked fettucine thoroughly and gently stir in the hot oil and bean mixture. Immediately stir in the diced Mozzarella cheese so that it starts to soften and melt before serving.

Fettucine con Fagioli

Gemelli con Feta
SPAGHETTI WITH FETA CHEESE AND BROWN BUTTER

350g/12 oz gemelli (plaited spaghetti)
1×15ml spoon/1 tablespoon olive oil
salt, freshly ground black pepper
75g/3 oz butter
50g/2 oz pitted black olives, chopped
175g/6 oz Feta cheese, coarsely crumbled
1×15ml spoon/1 tablespoon chopped fresh sage

Cook the gemelli in a large pan of steadily boiling water until *al dente* with the oil and 1×5ml spoon/1 teaspoon salt.

Meanwhile, melt the butter in a large pan and heat until it turns nutty brown in colour. Stir in the chopped olives, the Feta cheese, sage and salt and pepper to taste.

Drain the cooked pasta thoroughly and toss in the hot nutty butter until evenly coated. Serve immediately.

Lumache al Mascherpone e Noce
PASTA SNAILS WITH CREAM CHEESE AND WALNUTS

350g/12 oz lumache (pasta snails)
1×15ml spoon/1 tablespoon olive **or** walnut oil
salt, freshly ground black pepper
25g/1 oz butter
175g/6 oz full fat cream cheese
75g/3 oz walnuts, coarsely chopped

Cook the lumache in a large pan of steadily boiling water until *al dente* with the oil and 1×5ml spoon/1 teaspoon salt.

Meanwhile, melt the butter in a pan. Add the cream cheese and stir until melted and smooth. Season to taste with salt and pepper, and add the chopped walnuts.

Drain the cooked lumache thoroughly and toss in the cream cheese and walnut mixture. Serve immediately.

PASTA CON PESTO
PASTA WITH PESTO

2 medium potatoes, peeled and thinly sliced
salt, freshly ground black pepper
350g/12 oz fettucine
1 × 15ml spoon/1 tablespoon olive oil
2 × 15ml spoons/2 tablespoons butter, melted
2 × 15ml spoons/2 tablespoons Pesto (page 65)
1 × 15ml spoon/1 tablespoon poppy seeds

Cook the sliced potatoes in a pan of boiling salted water until just tender (they should still hold their shape).

Meanwhile, cook the fettucine in a large pan of steadily boiling water until *al dente* with the oil and 1 × 5ml spoon/1 teaspoon salt.

Drain the fettucine and potatoes thoroughly and toss lightly together with the melted butter, Pesto and poppy seeds. Serve immediately.

TORTELLINI ALLA PANNA
STUFFED PASTA TWISTS IN HERBED CREAM

350g/12 oz fresh tortellini (small stuffed pasta twists)
1 × 15ml spoon/1 tablespoon olive oil
salt, freshly ground black pepper
200ml/ ⅓ pint single cream
1 × 15ml spoon/1 tablespoon chopped fresh basil
1 × 15ml spoon/1 tablespoon chopped fresh tarragon
1 clove of garlic, crushed
a generous pinch of freshly grated nutmeg

Cook the tortellini in a large pan of steadily boiling water until *al dente* with the olive oil and 1 × 5ml spoon/1 teaspoon salt.

Meanwhile, heat the cream gently in a large shallow pan and add the chopped fresh herbs, the garlic, nutmeg and salt and pepper to taste.

Drain the cooked pasta thoroughly and stir it into the hot herbed cream. Heat through for 1–2 minutes.

Ravioli alla Piemontese
RAVIOLI WITH MUSHROOM AND TOMATO SAUCE

75g/3 oz butter
1 medium onion, thinly sliced
225g/8 oz button mushrooms, finely chopped
450g/1 lb Mediterranean tomatoes,
skinned, de-seeded and chopped
450ml/¾ pint Brodo di Manzo (beef stock, page 20)
350g/12 oz fresh ravioli
1 × 15ml spoon/1 tablespoon olive oil
salt, freshly ground black pepper

Melt half the butter in a pan and cook the onion, mushrooms and tomatoes until tender. Add the stock and simmer for 20 minutes.

Meanwhile, cook the ravioli in a large pan of steadily boiling water until *al dente* with the oil and 1 × 5ml spoon/1 teaspoon salt. Drain thoroughly. Melt the remaining butter and toss the ravioli in it. Off heat, add the sauce, and season to taste with salt and pepper. Mix thoroughly and serve immediately.

Fusilli alla Contadina
SPAGHETTI WITH BROCCOLI AND BREADCRUMB SAUCE

350g/12 oz fusilli (twisted spaghetti)
450g/1 lb broccoli, broken into florets
9 × 15ml spoons/9 tablespoons olive oil
salt, freshly ground black pepper
2 cloves garlic, chopped
5 anchovy fillets, drained and chopped
1 red chilli pepper
100g/4 oz freshly grated breadcrumbs

Cook the fusilli and broccoli in a large pan of steadily boiling water until *al dente* with 1 × 15ml spoon/1 tablespoon of the oil and 1 × 5ml spoon/1 teaspoon salt.

Meanwhile, heat 4 × 15ml spoons/4 tablespoons oil in a pan, add the garlic, three anchovy fillets and the chilli pepper. Cook until the garlic is golden-brown, then remove the chilli pepper.

Heat the remaining oil in a clean pan, add the breadcrumbs and the remaining anchovy fillets and cook until golden, stirring constantly.

Drain the pasta and broccoli thoroughly and place in a hot serving dish. Pour the oil and garlic mixture over the top, and sprinkle with the breadcrumb mixture. Season to taste with salt and pepper and serve immediately.

Fusilli alla Contadina

RIGATONI ROSSI
RIGATONI WITH SPICY RED SAUCE

25g/1 oz butter
2 × 15ml spoons/2 tablespoons olive oil
2 cloves garlic, finely chopped
450g/1 lb Mediterranean tomatoes,
skinned, de-seeded, and chopped
3 red chilli peppers, de-seeded and finely chopped
1 × 15ml spoon/1 tablespoon chopped fresh basil
salt, freshly ground black pepper
350g/12 oz rigatoni (ridge-shaped pasta tubes)
50g/2 oz Parmesan cheese, grated

Melt the butter in a pan with 1 × 15ml spoon/1 tablespoon of the olive oil and cook the chopped garlic until lightly golden. Add the tomatoes, chillis, basil and salt and pepper to taste, then simmer for 10–15 minutes until the sauce thickens.

Meanwhile, cook the rigatoni in a large pan of steadily boiling water until *al dente* with the remaining oil and 1 × 5ml spoon/1 teaspoon salt. Drain thoroughly, then stir gently into the hot sauce, together with the grated Parmesan cheese. Serve immediately.

RIGATONI CON POMODORI E FUNGHI SECCHI
RIGATONI WITH TOMATO SAUCE AND DRIED MUSHROOMS

25g/1 oz dried mushrooms
50g/2 oz butter
2 × 15ml spoons/2 tablespoons olive oil
1 small onion, finely chopped
25g/1 oz Italian ham, chopped
450g/1 lb Mediterranean tomatoes,
skinned, de-seeded and chopped
salt, freshly ground black pepper
350g/12 oz rigatoni (ridge-shaped pasta tubes)
75g/3 oz Fontina **or** Bel Paese cheese, diced

Put the dried mushrooms into a bowl and add sufficient water just to cover them; leave for 15 minutes. Drain the mushrooms, straining the soaking liquid and reserving it. Chop the plumped mushrooms.

Melt the butter and 1 × 15ml spoon/1 tablespoon olive oil in a pan and fry the onion gently until light golden. Add the chopped ham, tomatoes, salt and pepper to taste, the mushrooms and their strained liquid. Simmer the sauce for 10 minutes.

Meanwhile, cook the rigatoni in a large pan of steadily boiling water until *al dente* with the remaining olive oil and 1 × 5ml spoon/1 teaspoon salt. Drain thoroughly, then stir gently into the prepared hot sauce, together with the cheese. Serve immediately.

CONCHIGLIE ALLA CARRETTIERA
PASTA SHELLS WITH OLIVE, HERB AND CAPER SAUCE

350g/12 oz conchiglie (pasta shells)
8 × 15ml spoons/8 tablespoons olive oil
salt, freshly ground black pepper
1 large clove of garlic, crushed
1 × 2.5ml spoon/½ teaspoon ground ginger
3 × 15ml spoons/3 tablespoons capers
50g/2 oz black olives, pitted and sliced
50g/2 oz green olives, pitted and sliced
1 × 15ml spoon/1 tablespoon chopped parsley
1 × 15ml spoon/1 tablespoon chopped fresh thyme
1 × 15ml spoon/1 tablespoon raisins
1 × 15ml spoon/1 tablespoon chopped pine kernels

Cook the conchiglie in a large pan of steadily boiling water until *al dente* with 1 × 15ml spoon/1 tablespoon olive oil and 1 × 5ml spoon/1 teaspoon salt. Drain thoroughly. Put the remaining olive oil into a clean pan. Add the cooked pasta and stir in the olive oil. Add the remaining ingredients, season to taste and stir all together over gentle heat for 2 minutes until heated through. Serve immediately.

TAGLIATELLE ALLA ROMANA
TAGLIATELLE WITH PECORINO AND PEAS

350g/12 oz fresh peas, shelled
salt, freshly ground black pepper
350g/12 oz tagliatelle verde
1 × 15ml spoon/1 tablespoon olive oil
75g/3 oz butter, melted
75g/3 oz Pecorino cheese, grated
150ml/¼ pint double cream
100g/4 oz Italian ham, cut into thin strips

Cook the peas in a pan of boiling salted water until just tender.

Meanwhile, cook the tagliatelle in a large pan of steadily boiling water until *al dente* with the oil and 1 × 5ml spoon/1 teaspoon salt.

Drain the peas and the cooked tagliatelle thoroughly and gently stir into the butter over gentle heat. Stir in the Pecorino cheese, cream, strips of ham and salt and pepper to taste. Stir over gentle heat for 1 minute and serve immediately.

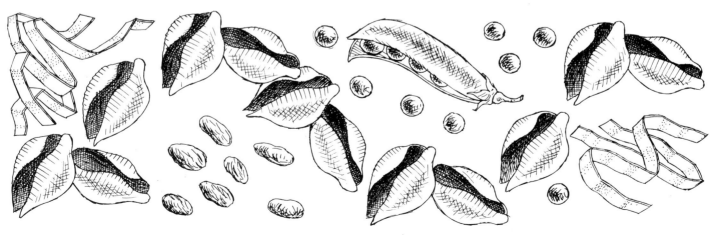

Pasta Salads

A pasta salad can be simple or elaborate, served as a starter, an accompaniment to a main course or even as a main course itself. The important thing to remember in each case is that it should have both shape and texture. Undercook the pasta slightly (by 1 minute) so that it keeps its natural shape. Drain it very well, then toss in a prepared dressing while it is still warm; the pasta then has a chance to absorb all the flavours, and the dressing prevents the pasta from sticking together.

Broad Bean and Pasta Salad

100g/4 oz lumache (pasta snails)
150ml/¼ pint olive oil
salt, freshly ground black pepper
1 large clove of garlic, crushed
2 × 15ml spoons/2 tablespoons chopped fresh sage
675g/1½ lb young broad beans, shelled
75g/3 oz Pecorino cheese, crumbled

Cook the lumache in a large pan of steadily boiling water until almost *al dente* with 1 × 15ml spoon/1 tablespoon olive oil and 1 × 5ml spoon/1 teaspoon salt.

Meanwhile, mix the remaining oil with salt and pepper to taste, the garlic and sage.

Drain the cooked pasta thoroughly, then stir in the dressing while the pasta is still warm. Leave to cool thoroughly, then stir in the shelled broad beans and the crumbled Pecorino cheese.

Serve as a starter.

Orange and Pasta Salad

175g/6 oz farfalle (pasta bows)
1 × 15ml spoon/1 tablespoon olive oil
salt, freshly ground black pepper
150ml/¼ pint soured cream
4 × 15ml spoons/4 tablespoons fresh orange juice
1 × 15ml spoon/1 tablespoon chopped fresh mint
2 large oranges, divided into segments
3 spring onions, finely chopped

GARNISH
orange slices
mint sprig

Cook the pasta in a large pan of steadily boiling water until almost *al dente* with the olive oil and 1 × 5ml spoon/1 teaspoon salt.

Meanwhile, mix the soured cream with salt and pepper to taste, the orange juice and the fresh mint.

Drain the cooked pasta thoroughly, then stir in the prepared dressing while the pasta is still warm. Leave to cool slightly, then stir in the orange segments and chopped spring onion. Garnish with the orange slices and sprig of mint. Do not chill but serve almost immediately.

Serve as a side salad.

Orange and Pasta Salad

ORIENTAL SALAD

4 large spring onions
100g/4 oz conchiglie (pasta shells)
7 × 15ml spoons/7 tablespoons olive oil
salt, freshly ground black pepper
juice of 1 orange
a pinch of ground ginger
3 × 5ml spoons/3 teaspoons soy sauce
1 large carrot, coarsely grated
100g/4 oz fresh bean shoots
¼ cucumber, quartered, de-seeded and diced
2 rings pineapple, fresh **or** canned, and chopped

Trim the spring onions to within 5cm/2 inches of their base. Cut each bulb piece of onion, at regular intervals lengthways, to within 1.25cm/½ inch of the base. Plunge the prepared onion bulbs into a bowl of iced water so that they open out into 'flowers'. Chop and reserve the top green ends of the spring onions.

Cook the conchiglie in a large pan of steadily boiling water until almost *al dente* with 1 × 15ml spoon/1 tablespoon of the olive oil and 1 × 5ml spoon/1 teaspoon salt.

Meanwhile, mix the remaining oil with the orange juice, ginger, soy sauce and salt and pepper to taste.

Drain the cooked pasta thoroughly, then stir in the prepared dressing while the pasta is still warm. Leave to cool, then add the carrot, bean shoots, cucumber, chopped pineapple and reserved chopped spring onion. Arrange the salad on a flat serving dish and garnish with the spring onion 'flowers'.

Serve as a side salad or as a main course.

PASTA WITH AVOCADO AND LEMON SAUCE

350g/12 oz conchiglie (pasta shells)
3 × 15ml spoons/3 tablespoons olive oil
salt, freshly ground black pepper
1 large ripe avocado pear, halved and stoned
grated rind and juice of 1 lemon
1 clove of garlic, crushed
2 × 5ml spoons/2 teaspoons sugar
3–4 × 15ml spoons/3–4 tablespoons milk
4 spring onions, chopped
2 × 15ml spoons/2 tablespoons chopped parsley

Cook the pasta in a large pan of steadily boiling water until almost *al dente* with 1 × 15ml spoon/1 tablespoon oil and 1 × 5ml spoon/1 teaspoon salt. Drain thoroughly and toss lightly in the remaining oil while still warm.

Meanwhile, scoop out the avocado flesh and blend until smooth with the lemon rind and juice, the salt and pepper, garlic, sugar and milk. Alternatively, mash the avocado and mix thoroughly with the other ingredients. Stir in the spring onions and parsley, thinning the sauce, if liked, with extra milk. Stir the avocado and lemon sauce into the pasta.

Serve as a starter or as a side salad.

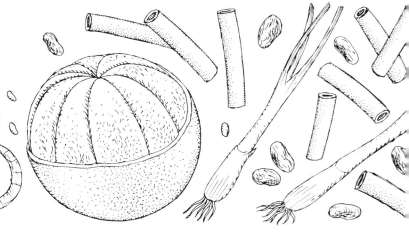

GINGERED PASTA SALAD

225g/8 oz stelline (star-shaped pasta)
4×15ml spoons/4 tablespoons olive oil
salt, freshly ground black pepper
juice of 1 lemon
2×5ml spoons/2 teaspoons finely shredded fresh ginger
75g/3 oz dried apricots, finely chopped
50g/2 oz sultanas
4 spring onions, chopped
1×15ml spoon/1 tablespoon chopped parsley

GARNISH
1 large orange, divided into segments

Cook the stelline in a large pan of steadily boiling water until almost *al dente* with 1×15ml spoon/1 tablespoon olive oil and 1×5ml spoon/1 teaspoon salt.

Mix the remaining oil with salt and pepper to taste, the lemon juice and the shredded ginger.

Drain the cooked pasta thoroughly, then stir in the dressing while the pasta is still warm, together with the chopped apricots and sultanas. Leave to cool, then stir in the spring onions and chopped parsley. Garnish with the orange segments.

Serve as a starter or as a side salad.

GARDEN PASTA SALAD

175g/6 oz penne (pasta tubes)
7×15ml spoons/7 tablespoons olive oil
salt, freshly ground black pepper
juice of 1 lemon
1×15ml spoon/1 tablespoon chopped parsley
1×15ml spoon/1 tablespoon chopped fresh basil
1×15ml spoon/1 tablespoon chopped watercress
1×15ml spoon/1 tablespoon concentrated
tomato purée
a generous pinch of caster sugar
2 carrots, very thinly sliced
2 courgettes, very thinly sliced
1 small onion, cut into thin rings
1 medium leek, cut into matchstick strips
4 radishes, thinly sliced

Cook the pasta in a large pan of steadily boiling water until almost *al dente* with 1×15ml spoon/1 tablespoon olive oil and 1×5ml spoon/1 teaspoon salt.

Meanwhile, mix the lemon juice with the remaining olive oil, the parsley, basil, watercress, tomato purée and caster sugar. Add seasoning to taste.

Drain the cooked pasta thoroughly, then stir in the prepared dressing while the pasta is still warm. Leave to cool thoroughly, then stir in the sliced carrots, courgettes, onion rings, leek strips and sliced radishes.

Serve as a starter or as a side salad.

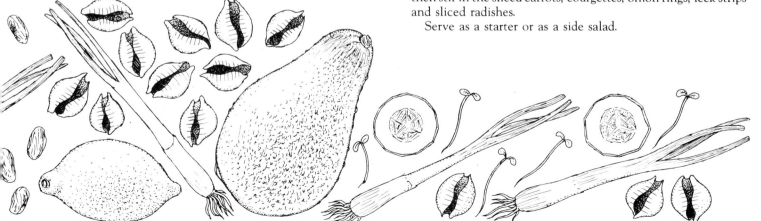

Pesto Pasta Salad

350g/12 oz rigatoni (ridge-shaped pasta tubes)
1 × 15ml spoon/1 tablespoon olive oil
salt, freshly ground black pepper
4 × 15ml spoons/4 tablespoons Pesto (page 65)
5 sticks celery, chopped
1 medium red pepper, de-seeded and diced
1 bunch of spring onions, chopped
350g/12 oz canned sweetcorn kernels, drained

GARNISH
100g/4 oz button mushrooms, sliced

Cook the rigatoni in a large pan of steadily boiling water until almost *al dente* with the oil and 1 × 5ml spoon/1 teaspoon salt. Drain thoroughly, then gently stir in the Pesto while the pasta is still warm. Leave to cool, then add the celery, red pepper, spring onions and sweetcorn, and mix together well. Arrange the salad on a plate and garnish with the mushrooms.

Serve as a side salad.

Pasta, Bean and Tuna Salad

225g/8 oz maccheroni rigati (ridged macaroni)
7 × 15ml spoons/7 tablespoons olive oil
salt, freshly ground black pepper
2 × 15ml spoons/2 tablespoons white wine vinegar
1 × 15ml spoon/1 tablespoon chopped chives
1 clove of garlic, crushed
finely grated rind of $\frac{1}{2}$ lemon
5 × 15ml spoons/5 tablespoons canned
red kidney beans
200g/7 oz canned tuna fish in brine,
drained and coarsely flaked
4 anchovy fillets, drained and
split lengthways (optional)

Cook the pasta in a large pan of steadily boiling water until almost *al dente* with 1 × 15ml spoon/1 tablespoon olive oil and 1 × 5ml spoon/1 teaspoon salt.

Meanwhile, mix the remaining olive oil with the vinegar, chives, garlic, lemon rind and salt and pepper to taste.

Drain the cooked pasta thoroughly, then stir in the prepared dressing while the pasta is still warm. Leave to cool, then stir in the kidney beans and the tuna fish. Arrange the anchovy fillets on top, if used.

Serve as a starter or as a main course.

Pasta, Bean and Tuna Salad

PASTA AND TUNA SALAD

175g/6 oz elbow maccheroni
1 × 15ml spoon/1 tablespoon olive oil
salt, freshly ground black pepper

SAUCE
200g/7 oz canned tuna fish in brine **or** oil
6 anchovy fillets, drained
200ml/⅓ pint Maionese (page 65)
juice of 1 lemon
1 × 15ml spoon/1 tablespoon capers
1 clove of garlic, crushed
2 × 15ml spoons/2 tablespoons chopped parsley
white wine, Brodo di Pollo (chicken stock, page 19)
or milk (see Method)

GARNISH
extra capers
extra anchovy fillets, drained
small lemon wedges

Cook the pasta in a large pan of steadily boiling water until almost *al dente* with the oil and 1 × 5ml spoon/1 teaspoon salt.

Meanwhile, put the tuna fish into a liquidizer with the anchovy fillets, Maionese, lemon juice, capers, garlic and parsley. Blend until smooth. Alternatively, pound the fish and mix with the other sauce ingredients. If the sauce seems very thick, add a little white wine, chicken stock or milk.

Drain the cooked pasta thoroughly, then stir in the prepared sauce while the pasta is still warm. Chill for 1–2 hours.

Spoon the salad into a serving dish and garnish with extra capers, a criss-cross of anchovy fillets and small lemon wedges.

Serve as a starter.

Variation
Add a few peeled prawns to the salad.

MIMOSA PASTA SALAD

225g/8 oz conchiglie (pasta shells)
5 × 15ml spoons/5 tablespoons olive oil
salt, freshly ground black pepper
grated rind and juice of 1 lemon
200ml/⅓ pint Maionese (page 65)
225g/8 oz cooked smoked haddock, flaked
3 × 15ml spoons/3 tablespoons capers
2 hard-boiled eggs
2 × 15ml spoons/2 tablespoons chopped parsley

Cook the conchiglie in a large pan of steadily boiling water until almost *al dente* with 1 × 15ml spoon/1 tablespoon olive oil and 1 × 5ml spoon/1 teaspoon salt.

Meanwhile, mix together the remaining olive oil with the lemon rind and juice and salt and pepper to taste.

Drain the pasta thoroughly, then stir in the prepared dressing while the pasta is still warm. Leave to cool, then mix in the Maionese, flaked haddock and capers. Separate the whites and yolks from the hard-boiled eggs. Chop the whites finely, and sieve the yolks. Stir the chopped egg white into the pasta mixture and spoon into a serving dish. Sprinkle with the chopped parsley and then with the sieved hard-boiled egg yolk.

Serve as a side salad or as a main course.

Sweet Sour Pasta and Chicken Salad

1 medium aubergine, cut into 1.25cm/½ inch cubes
salt, freshly ground black pepper
175g/6 oz wholewheat pasta rings
150ml/¼ pint olive oil
3 × 15ml spoons/3 tablespoons white wine vinegar
6 × 15ml spoons/6 tablespoons tomato juice
a squeeze of lemon juice
1 × 15ml spoon/1 tablespoon caster sugar
1 clove of garlic, chopped
225g/8 oz cooked chicken, chopped

Put the aubergine cubes into a colander and sprinkle generously with salt, then leave to drain for 30 minutes.

Meanwhile, cook the pasta rings in a large pan of steadily boiling water until almost *al dente* with 1 × 15ml spoon/1 tablespoon of the oil and 1 × 5ml spoon/1 teaspoon salt.

Mix the vinegar with the tomato juice, 4 × 15ml spoons/ 4 tablespoons olive oil, the lemon juice, caster sugar, garlic and salt and pepper to taste.

Pat the aubergine dry on absorbent paper. Put the remaining oil in a pan and fry the aubergine gently until lightly golden. (If the aubergine is very porous, it may require a little extra oil.)

Drain the pasta thoroughly, then stir in the prepared dressing together with the fried aubergine cubes and the chopped chicken. Chill thoroughly before serving.

Serve as a starter or as a main course.

Chicken and Artichoke Salad

175g/6 oz farfalle (pasta bows)
7 × 15ml spoons/7 tablespoons olive oil
salt, freshly ground black pepper
2 × 15ml spoons/2 tablespoons white wine vinegar
2 × 15ml spoons/2 tablespoons chopped parsley
1 clove of garlic, crushed
1 × 5ml spoon/1 teaspoon French mustard
175g/6 oz smoked chicken, divided into strips
(see **Note**)
6 canned artichoke hearts, quartered
3 × 15ml spoons/3 tablespoons soured cream

GARNISH
paprika

Cook the farfalle in a large pan of steadily boiling water until almost *al dente* with 1 × 15ml spoon/1 tablespoon of the oil and 1 × 5ml spoon/1 teaspoon salt.

Meanwhile, mix the remaining olive oil with the vinegar, salt and pepper to taste, the parsley, garlic and mustard.

Drain the cooked farfalle thoroughly, then stir in the prepared dressing while the pasta is still warm. Leave to cool, then mix in the strips of chicken and quartered artichoke hearts. Spoon the salad into a serving dish and top with the soured cream. Sprinkle with paprika.

Serve as a side salad or as a main course.

Note Smoked chicken is obtainable from good delicatessens. Use plainly cooked chicken if smoked chicken is not available.

ITALIAN HAM AND PASTA SALAD

Serves 6

225g/8 oz anelli (pasta rings)
1 × 15ml spoon/1 tablespoon olive oil
salt, freshly ground black pepper
150ml/¼ pint soured cream
1 × 15ml spoon/1 tablespoon lemon juice
1 × 15ml spoon/1 tablespoon chopped chives
225g/8 oz Italian ham, chopped
2 oranges, divided into segments
100g/4 oz cooked broad beans

GARNISH
grated orange rind

Cook the pasta in a large pan of steadily boiling water until almost *al dente* with the oil and 1 × 5ml spoon/1 teaspoon salt.

Meanwhile, mix together the soured cream, lemon juice and chopped chives, and season to taste.

Drain the pasta thoroughly and toss in the dressing while still warm. Leave to cool, then add the ham, orange segments and beans, and adjust seasoning to taste. Garnish with the orange rind.

Serve as a starter or as a main course.

SMOKED SALMON AND AVOCADO PASTA SALAD

225g/8 oz conchiglie (pasta shells)
7 × 15ml spoons/7 tablespoons olive oil
salt, freshly ground black pepper
3 × 15ml spoons/3 tablespoons lemon juice
1 × 2.5ml spoon/½ teaspoon French mustard
100g/4 oz smoked salmon, sliced into thin strips
100g/4 oz peeled prawns
1 large avocado pear, peeled, stoned and scooped into balls
6 spring onions, finely chopped
1 × 15ml spoon/1 tablespoon chopped parsley

GARNISH
unpeeled prawns
lettuce leaves

Cook the pasta in a large pan of steadily boiling water until almost *al dente* with 1 × 15ml spoon/1 tablespoon oil and 1 × 5ml spoon/1 teaspoon salt.

Meanwhile, mix together the lemon juice, remaining oil, the mustard and salt and pepper to taste.

Drain the pasta thoroughly and stir in the prepared dressing. Leave to cool, then add the salmon, prawns, avocado, spring onions and chopped parsley. Garnish with unpeeled prawns and serve on a bed of lettuce.

Serve as a starter.

Smoked Salmon and Avocado Pasta Salad

PASTA SAUCES

This is one of the most important chapters in the book, as a sauce that is served with pasta can either make or mar the finished dish.

The sauces of Italy, particularly those that are often served with pasta, differ greatly from the sauces of most other countries. With some exceptions, few are thickened with flour, and many savoury ones are based on olive oil. Cream is added to savoury sauces less frequently than it is to sweet sauces.

The best known sauce has to be *Bolognese*, sometimes referred to as *Ragu* (see page 29 – Spaghetti Bolognese). This classic meat sauce is traditionally served with spaghetti, but can accompany almost any cooked pasta.

Some sauces can be frozen. It is important, however, to thaw them completely before use. Re-heat in a double saucepan or in a basin over a pan of hot water. As many separate upon being chilled or thawed, they should be stirred before being re-heated.

SALSA BESCIAMELLA
SAVOURY WHITE SAUCE

Makes 600ml/1 pint (approx)

750ml/1¼ pints milk
2 bay leaves
1 small onion, peeled and stuck with 2 cloves
a small sprig of fresh thyme
40g/1½ oz butter
40g/1½ oz plain flour
salt, freshly ground black pepper
a generous pinch of ground mace

Put the milk into a pan with the bay leaves, onion and cloves and the thyme. Bring to the boil slowly, then cover the pan and leave to stand, off the heat, for about 45 minutes.

Melt the butter in a clean pan. Stir in the flour and cook gently for 1 minute, stirring all the time. Add the strained flavoured milk slowly, beating well between each addition. Once all the milk has been incorporated, bring the sauce to the boil. Reduce the heat and simmer gently for 10–15 minutes until the sauce has thickened and reduced slightly. Season to taste with salt, pepper and mace.

Use for baked pasta dishes.

Note This sauce can be made 24 hours in advance and kept chilled. It can be frozen for up to 6 months.

Variation
For a thicker sauce, either add a little extra flour to the melted butter, or simmer the sauce for longer. (The longer the sauce is cooked, the greater will be the depth of flavour. Take care, however, that it does not burn.)

MAIONESE
ITALIAN MAYONNAISE

Makes 450ml/¾ pint (approx)

3 egg yolks
1 × 15ml spoon/1 tablespoon white wine vinegar
300ml/½ pint olive oil
1 clove of garlic, crushed
salt, freshly ground black pepper
2 × 15ml spoons/2 tablespoons chopped fresh basil
1–2 × 15ml spoons/1–2 tablespoons hot water
(see Method)

Whisk the egg yolks in a bowl to break them up. Whisk in the white wine vinegar, and then gradually add the olive oil in a fine trickle, whisking all the time, until all the olive oil has been incorporated. Add the garlic, salt and pepper to taste and the fresh basil. If the mayonnaise is too thick, thin to the desired consistency with a little hot water.

Use for pasta salads.

Note Maionese can be chilled for up to 24 hours in a covered container. It should not be frozen.

PESTO
HERB AND PINE KERNEL SAUCE

Makes 300ml/½ pint (approx)

a good sized bunch of fresh basil leaves
4 garlic cloves, peeled
40g/1½ oz pine kernels
salt, freshly ground black pepper
200ml/ ⅓ pint olive oil

Trim off the excess stalks from the basil leaves. Put the leaves into a liquidizer or food processor with the garlic, pine kernels, salt and pepper to taste and half the olive oil. Blend until smooth and then gradually add the remaining olive oil.

Use for plainly cooked pasta. Stir into cooked tagliatelle or fettucine.

Note Pesto is traditionally made with a pestle and mortar. The basil, garlic, pine kernels and seasoning are ground until they form a paste. The oil is then gradually added, a little at a time, until the sauce is smooth.

Pesto can be stored in a covered container in a refrigerator for up to 1 week. It is not suitable for freezing.

Variation
If preparing Pesto manually, substitute ground almonds for the pine kernels. Finely chop the basil, crush the garlic and mix the ingredients together.

SALSA DI DRAGONCELLO
TARRAGON SAUCE

Makes 300ml/½ pint (approx)

2 × 15ml spoons/2 tablespoons chopped fresh tarragon
7 × 15ml spoons/7 tablespoons Brodo di Pollo
(chicken stock, page 19)
7 × 15ml spoons/7 tablespoons dry white wine
salt, freshly ground black pepper
6 × 15ml spoons/6 tablespoons spinach purée
(frozen chopped spinach can be used)
75g/3 oz butter
freshly grated nutmeg

Put the chopped tarragon, chicken stock, wine and salt and pepper to taste into a pan. Bring to the boil and boil steadily until the liquid has almost evaporated. Add the spinach purée and heat through.

Melt the butter in a pan until it turns golden; do not allow it to burn. Beat the butter into the tarragon and spinach purée, and season with the nutmeg. Heat through but do not allow the sauce to boil.

Use for cooked short cut and shaped pastas.

Note This sauce should be used fresh. It is not suitable for storage.

SALSA DI FEGATINI
CHICKEN LIVER SAUCE

Makes 450ml/¾ pint sauce

40g/1½ oz butter
1 small onion, finely chopped
225g/8 oz chicken livers, chopped finely
25g/1 oz plain flour
100g/4 oz button mushrooms, finely chopped
7 × 15ml spoons/7 tablespoons Brodo di Manzo
(beef stock, page 20)
7 × 15ml spoons/7 tablespoons red wine
4 × 15ml spoons/4 tablespoons Marsala
juice of 1 orange
salt, freshly ground black pepper

Melt the butter in a pan and gently fry the chopped onion for 4–5 minutes. Add the chicken livers and fry gently until sealed on all sides. Sprinkle the flour over the chicken livers, stirring it in. Add the mushrooms and gradually stir in the beef stock, wine, Marsala and orange juice. Simmer until the livers are tender and the sauce very thick. Season to taste with salt and pepper.

Serve as a topping sauce for plainly cooked pasta.

Note This sauce can be chilled for 24 hours and frozen for 1 month.

Salsa Genovese
GENOESE VEAL SAUCE

Makes 400ml/⅔ pint (approx)

40g/1½ oz butter
1 medium onion, thinly sliced
3 stalks celery, finely chopped
1 large carrot, finely chopped
225g/8 oz lean veal, finely chopped **or** minced
1 clove of garlic, crushed
1×15ml spoon/1 tablespoon flour
150ml/¼ pint red wine
150ml/¼ pint Brodo di Manzo (beef stock, page 20)
salt, freshly ground black pepper
2×5ml spoons/2 tablespoons Pesto (page 65)

Melt the butter in a pan and gently fry the onion for 4–5 minutes. Add the celery, carrot and veal, and fry until the meat is evenly browned. Stir in the garlic and the flour. Gradually add the wine and stock, and bring to the boil. Season to taste with salt and pepper and add the Pesto. Reduce the heat and simmer the sauce for 20–25 minutes.

Use for plainly cooked long pasta.

Note This sauce can be chilled for 24 hours. It can be frozen for 1 month.

Variation
Soak 1×15ml spoon/1 tablespoon chopped or sliced dried mushrooms in warm water for 15 minutes. Drain well and add to the sauce when frying the celery, carrot and veal.

Salsa di Gamberi
PRAWN SAUCE

Makes 300ml/½ pint (approx)

225g/8 oz unshelled prawns
a sprig of fresh fennel **or** 1×2.5ml spoon/½ teaspoon dried fennel
300ml/½ pint dry white wine
a strip of lemon rind
150ml/¼ pint Italian dry vermouth
salt, freshly ground black pepper
25g/1 oz butter
1 small onion, finely chopped
1×15ml spoon/1 tablespoon flour
4×15ml spoons/4 tablespoons double cream
2×15ml spoons/2 tablespoons chopped parsley

Shell the prawns and put to one side. Put the shells into a pan with the fennel, white wine, lemon rind, vermouth and salt and pepper to taste. Simmer until the liquid has reduced by one-third, then strain it.

Melt the butter in a pan and gently fry the onion for 3–4 minutes. Stir in the flour and cook for 1 minute. Gradually add the prawn liquid, stirring constantly. Bring to the boil, then reduce the heat and simmer the sauce for 2–3 minutes. Stir in the cream, the reserved prawns and chopped parsley and heat through.

Use for cooked pasta shapes.

Note This sauce should be used fresh. It is not suitable for storage.

SALSA ALLA VENETA
VENETIAN LOBSTER SAUCE

Makes 200ml/⅓ pint (approx)

6 × 15ml spoons/6 tablespoons olive oil
3 cloves garlic, finely chopped
100g/4 oz chopped cooked lobster meat
6 anchovy fillets, drained and chopped
2 × 15ml spoons/2 tablespoons chopped parsley
1 × 15ml spoon/1 tablespoon red wine vinegar
salt, freshly ground black pepper

Heat the oil in a pan and gently fry the chopped garlic for 1 minute. Add the remaining ingredients and boil quite quickly for 1–2 minutes until reduced.
Use for cooked pasta shells.

Note   This sauce should be used immediately. It is not suitable for storage.

SALSA DI VONGOLE
CLAM SAUCE

Makes 750ml/1¼ pints (approx)

1 × 15ml spoon/1 tablespoon olive oil
1 onion, finely chopped
250g/9 oz canned clams, drained
450g/1 lb Mediterranean tomatoes,
skinned, de-seeded and chopped
1 × 5ml spoon/1 teaspoon fresh mixed herbs
150ml/¼ pint white wine
salt, freshly ground black pepper

Heat the oil in a pan and cook the onion until soft. Add the clams, chopped tomatoes, herbs and wine, and season to taste with salt and pepper. Simmer the sauce for 5 minutes.
Use for cooked long pasta.

Note   This sauce should be used fresh. It is not suitable for storage.

SALSA AGRODOLCE
ITALIAN SWEET AND SOUR SAUCE

Makes 300ml/½ pint (approx)

40g/1½ oz butter
1 large onion, finely chopped
2 × 15ml spoons/2 tablespoons flour
150ml/¼ pint Brodo di Manzo (beef stock, page 20)
150ml/¼ pint red wine
3 × 15ml spoons/3 tablespoons Marsala
3 × 15ml spoons/3 tablespoons white wine vinegar
finely grated rind of ½ orange
25g/1 oz sultanas
1 × 15ml spoon/1 tablespoon pine kernels, chopped
2 × 15ml spoons/2 tablespoons granulated sugar
3 × 15ml spoons/3 tablespoons water
25g/1 oz dark plain chocolate, grated
salt, freshly ground black pepper

Melt the butter in a pan and gently fry the onion for 4 minutes. Stir in the flour and cook for 1 minute. Gradually stir in the beef stock and wine, and bring to the boil. Add the Marsala, white wine vinegar, orange rind, sultanas and pine kernels, reduce the heat and simmer for 15 minutes.

Meanwhile, put the sugar and water into a small pan and stir over gentle heat until the sugar has dissolved. Boil steadily until the syrup turns caramel in colour. Stir the caramel into the sauce, together with the grated chocolate and salt and pepper to taste. Heat the sauce through until the chocolate has melted and the sauce is glossy.

Use for plainly cooked shaped pasta. Alternatively, spoon the sauce over cooked noodles when serving them as an accompaniment to cooked poultry or game.

Note   This sauce should be used fresh. It is not suitable for storage.

AGLIATA
GARLIC AND BREADCRUMB SAUCE

Makes 200ml/⅓ pint (approx)

3 garlic cloves, crushed
4×15ml spoons/4 tablespoons fresh white breadcumbs
1×15ml spoon/1 tablespoon white wine vinegar
salt, freshly ground black pepper
150ml/¼ pint olive oil

Put the crushed garlic, breadcrumbs, vinegar and salt and pepper to taste into a bowl. Mix in the olive oil until the sauce is smooth.

Use for plainly cooked pasta. Stir into cooked tagliatelle or fettucine.

Note Agliata can be chilled for 3–4 days. It is not suitable for freezing.

SALSA VERDE AL RAFANO
GREEN HORSERADISH SAUCE

Makes 300ml/½ pint (approx)

350g/12 oz Mediterranean tomatoes,
skinned, de-seeded and chopped
1 clove of garlic, crushed
3×15ml spoons/3 tablespoons fine fresh breadcrumbs
2×15ml spoons/2 tablespoons chopped parsley
1×15ml spoon/1 tablespoon finely chopped mint
1×15ml spoon/1 tablespoon freshly grated horseradish
150ml/¼ pint olive oil (approx)
salt, freshly ground black pepper

Mix the chopped tomatoes with the garlic, breadcrumbs, parsley, mint and horseradish. Beat in the oil until it is evenly absorbed. Add more oil if a thinner sauce is required. Season to taste with salt and pepper.

Use for pasta salads.

Note This sauce should be used fresh. It is not suitable for storage.

SALSA DI GORGONZOLA
CREAMY GORGONZOLA SAUCE

Makes 450ml/¾ pint (approx)

300ml/½ pint double cream
2×15ml spoons/2 tablespoons Marsala
175g/6 oz Gorgonzola, finely crumbled
1 clove of garlic, crushed
salt, freshly ground black pepper

Put the cream into a pan with the Marsala, and heat through. Add the Gorgonzola and stir over gentle heat until the cheese has dissolved and the sauce is creamy. Stir in the garlic and add salt and pepper to taste.

Use for plainly cooked long pasta.

Note This sauce can be chilled for 24 hours. It is not suitable for freezing.

SALSA DI NOCI
WALNUT AND PARSLEY SAUCE

Makes 300ml/½ pint (approx)

75g/3 oz ground walnuts
50g/2 oz butter, melted
3×15ml spoons/3 tablespoons fine fresh breadcrumbs
4×15ml spoons/4 tablespoons finely chopped parsley
150ml/¼ pint olive oil
salt, freshly ground black pepper
3×15ml spoons/3 tablespoons double cream
a pinch of grated nutmeg

Mix the ground walnuts with the melted butter and the breadcrumbs. Stir in the parsley and gradually beat in the oil. Add salt and pepper to taste, the cream and nutmeg. Blend in a liquidizer or food processor if a very smooth sauce is required.

Serve cold with plainly cooked hot pasta – home-made tagliatelle or fettucine are perfect choices.

Note This sauce should be used fresh. It is not suitable for storage.

BAGNA CAUDA
GARLIC AND OLIVE OIL SAUCE

Makes 300ml/½ pint (approx)

150ml/¼ pint olive oil
100g/4 oz butter
8 anchovy fillets, drained and finely chopped
2–3 cloves garlic, crushed
freshly ground black pepper

Put the oil and butter into a small flameproof casserole or fondue pot. Stand over the heat and stir until the butter and oil are evenly melted and hot. Add the anchovy fillets, garlic and pepper to taste (salt is not necessary), and stir.

Serve piping hot with cooked pasta shapes.

Note   This sauce is traditionally served in the Piedmont region of Italy in the same way as a fondue; the sauce is put into a small flameproof pan over a table burner, and surrounded by a selection of raw vegetables to use as dunks. It is equally delicious however, if cooked pasta shapes are served as accompanying dunks. It should be used fresh.

SALSA ROSSA
RED SAUCE

Makes 300ml/½ pint (approx)

3 × 15ml spoons/3 tablespoons olive oil
1 large onion, thinly sliced
2 medium green peppers, de-seeded and thinly sliced
450g/1 lb Mediterranean tomatoes,
skinned, de-seeded and chopped
½ × 2.5ml spoon/¼ teaspoon chilli powder
salt
Brodo di Manzo (beef stock, page 20) **or**
red wine (see Method)

Heat the oil in a pan and gently fry the onion for 3–4 minutes. Add the peppers and tomatoes, and cook gently until the vegetables become soft and squashy. Add the chilli powder and salt to taste, and simmer the sauce for 5–10 minutes. This sauce is naturally very thick but it can be thinned by the addition of stock or red wine.

Use for cooked long or shaped pastas.

Note   This sauce can be chilled for 24 hours. It can be frozen for 6 months.

Bagna Cauda

Sugo di Pomodoro e Panna
TOMATO AND CREAM SAUCE

Makes 600ml/1 pint (approx)

100g/4 oz butter
1 medium onion, finely chopped
1 medium carrot, finely chopped
2 sticks celery, finely chopped
675g/1½lb ripe Mediterranean tomatoes,
skinned, de-seeded and roughly chopped
150ml/¼ pint Brodo di Pollo (chicken stock, page 19)
or dry white wine
1 clove of garlic, crushed
salt, freshly ground black pepper
a pinch of caster sugar
1 × 15ml spoon/1 tablespoon chopped fresh basil
2 × 15ml spoons/2 tablespoons
concentrated tomato purée
150ml/¼ pint double cream

Melt the butter in a pan and gently fry the onion, carrot and celery for 5 minutes until soft. Stir in the other ingredients apart from the cream, and bring to the boil. Reduce the heat and simmer gently for 20 minutes.

Blend the sauce in a liquidizer or food processor, or sieve it until smooth. Return to a clean pan and stir in the cream. Heat through gently and adjust seasoning to taste.

Serve as a topping sauce or use for baked pasta dishes.

Note   This sauce can be chilled for 2 hours. It can be frozen for 6 months.

Salsa di Pomodoro
FRESH TOMATO SAUCE

Makes 450ml/¾ pint (approx)

1kg/2¼lb Mediterranean tomatoes, roughly chopped
1 medium onion, finely chopped
1 large carrot, chopped
3 stalks celery, finely chopped
2 cloves garlic, crushed
1 × 15ml spoon/1 tablespoon chopped fresh thyme
1 × 15ml spoon/1 tablespoon chopped fresh basil
1 × 5ml spoon/1 teaspoon caster sugar
2 × 15ml spoons/2 tablespoons
concentrated tomato purée
salt, freshly ground black pepper
Brodo di Pollo (chicken stock, page 19)

Put all the ingredients into a large pan. Cover, and bring to the boil, then reduce the heat and simmer gently for about 30 minutes until the tomatoes are pulpy and all the other vegetables quite soft.

Sieve the sauce, then re-heat to serve, adjusting the consistency by adding a little chicken stock, if liked.

Serve as a topping sauce or use for baked pasta dishes.

Note   This sauce can be chilled for 24 hours. It can be frozen for 6 months.

Variation
Add 1–2 × 5ml spoons/1–2 teaspoons anchovy essence and 8 anchovy fillets, drained and finely chopped to the above quantity of prepared sauce.

SALSA DI ARANCI
WHISKED ORANGE SAUCE

Makes 300ml/½ pint (approx)

6 egg yolks
2 × 15ml spoons/2 tablespoons orange flower water
50g/2 oz caster sugar
3 × 15ml spoons/3 tablespoons double cream

Whisk the egg yolks with the orange flower water and sugar until light and creamy. Put into the top of a double saucepan, or in a basin over a pan of hot water. Add the cream, then stir the sauce over gentle heat until it is thick enough to coat the back of a wooden spoon. Remove the pan from the heat and serve the sauce immediately poured over the top of freshly cooked pasta.

Note Serve fresh. This sauce is not suitable for storage.

SALSA DI CIOCCOLATO
ITALIAN CHOCOLATE SAUCE

Makes 400ml/⅔ pint (approx)

300ml/½ pint single cream
75g/3 oz plain chocolate
2 × 15ml spoons/2 tablespoons Amaretto liqueur
25g/1 oz butter
1 × 15ml spoon/1 tablespoon flour
1 × 15ml spoon/1 tablespoon vanilla sugar
2 egg yolks

Put the cream and chocolate into a saucepan and stir over very gentle heat until the chocolate has melted. Remove from the heat, stir in the Amaretto and leave to cool.

Melt the butter in a pan, then stir in the flour and cook gently for 1 minute. Gradually stir in the cream and melted chocolate. Bring to the boil and stir until the sauce has thickened. Stir in the sugar, beat in the egg yolks, and heat the sauce through without allowing it to boil. Use for plainly cooked pasta.

Note Serve fresh. This sauce is not suitable for storage.

SALSA DI PESCHE E AMARETTI
PEACH AND MACAROON SAUCE

Makes 400ml/⅔ pint (approx)

3 large, ripe peaches
50g/2 oz caster sugar
8 Amaretti (small macaroons), finely crushed
finely grated rind of ½ orange
200ml/⅓ pint single cream

Nick the skin at the stalk end of each peach. Plunge into a bowl of boiling water for 45 seconds, then remove the peaches and slide off the skins. Cut each peach around the middle; twist to separate the two halves, then remove the stones. Sieve the flesh, then mix the purée with the sugar, Amaretti, orange rind and cream. Use for cooked long or shaped pasta.

Note Serve fresh. This sauce is not suitable for storage.

SALSA DI STREGA
STREGA SAUCE

Makes 225g/8 oz (approx)

100g/4 oz unsalted butter
100g/4 oz soft brown sugar
3 × 15ml spoons/3 tablespoons Strega liqueur
25g/1 oz ground almonds
finely grated rind of ½ lemon
a generous pinch of ground cinnamon

Beat the butter until it is soft and light, then beat in the sugar and Strega until soft and smooth. Add the ground almonds, lemon rind and cinnamon, and mix together well.

Serve on top of freshly cooked pasta, or as below.

Note This is really a sweet 'butter'. Make it up in advance, cover with waxed paper and roll up. Store in a refrigerator or freezer for 2–3 days. It is then ready for melting and tossing with cooked noodles or pasta shapes for a quick pudding.

Sweet Pasta Recipes

Pasta is just as versatile when used in a sweet context as it is in a savoury one; indeed, it was particularly popular in the eighteenth and nineteenth centuries when it was often eaten with sticky sweet sauces.

A simple way of presenting a sweet pasta dish is to cook the pasta in exactly the same way as for savoury recipes, then to top or mix it with a sweet sauce, cream or nuts. Alternatively, it can merely be tossed in melted butter with the addition of sugar and spices.

Remember to precede pasta desserts with a light main course.

Tagliatelle with Kiwi Fruit

225g/8 oz tagliatelle
1 × 15ml spoon/1 tablespoon olive oil
1 × 5ml spoon/1 teaspoon salt
40g/1½ oz butter
rind and juice of 1 large orange
2 × 15ml spoons/2 tablespoons granulated sugar
1 × 15ml spoon/1 tablespoon brandy

DECORATION
2 kiwi fruit, peeled and sliced
1 × 15ml spoon/1 tablespoon flaked almonds,
lightly toasted

Cook the tagliatelle in a large pan of steadily boiling water until *al dente* with the olive oil and salt.

Meanwhile, melt the butter in a pan over gentle heat, then add the orange rind and juice and the sugar, and stir until the sugar has dissolved. Stir in the brandy and heat through.

Drain the cooked tagliatelle thoroughly and toss quickly with the hot orange butter. Transfer to a serving dish and decorate with the sliced kiwi fruit and the flaked almonds.

Serve with whipped cream.

Tagliatelle with Kiwi Fruit

TAGLIATELLE WITH STRAWBERRY SAUCE

350g/12 oz strawberries, hulled and halved
50g/2 oz vanilla sugar **or** caster sugar
juice of 1 lemon
3 × 15ml spoons/3 tablespoons Cointreau
225g/8 oz tagliatelle
1 × 15ml spoon/1 tablespoon olive oil
1 × 5ml spoon/1 teaspoon salt
150ml/¼ pint single cream

DECORATION
2 × 15ml spoons/2 tablespoons flaked almonds, lightly toasted

Put the strawberries into a shallow dish and sprinkle with the sugar, lemon juice and Cointreau. Cover and chill for 2–3 hours.

Meanwhile, cook the tagliatelle in a large pan of steadily boiling water until *al dente* with the oil and salt. Drain thoroughly and toss over gentle heat with the single cream. Transfer the pasta to a serving dish and top with the chilled strawberries and their juices. Sprinkle with the toasted almonds and serve immediately.

SEVILLE SHELL PUDDING

225g/8 oz conchiglie (pasta shells)
1 × 15ml spoon/1 tablespoon olive oil
1 × 5ml spoon/1 teaspoon salt
juice of 2 oranges
finely grated rind of 1 orange
50g/2 oz butter
50g/2 oz granulated sugar
4 × 15ml spoons/4 tablespoons double cream
1 large orange, divided into segments

DECORATION
2 × 15ml spoons/2 tablespoons chopped hazelnuts

Cook the pasta shells in a large pan of steadily boiling water until *al dente* with the olive oil and salt.

Meanwhile, put the orange juice into a pan with the orange rind, butter, sugar and double cream. Stir over gentle heat until the sugar has dissolved and the mixture is well blended. Add the orange segments.

Drain the cooked pasta shells thoroughly and stir into the hot orange sauce. Transfer to a serving dish and sprinkle with the hazelnuts. Serve immediately with ice cream.

Note This recipe is particularly delicious when accompanied by chocolate ice cream.

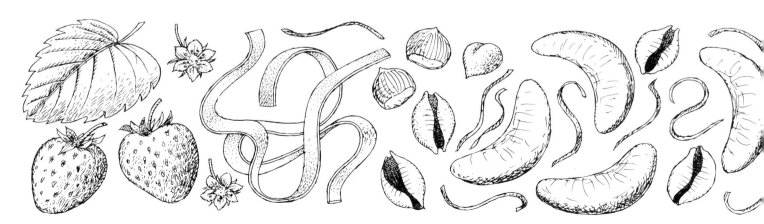

JUBILEE PASTA

225g/8 oz lumache (pasta snails)
1 × 15ml spoon/1 tablespoon olive oil
1 × 5ml spoon/1 teaspoon salt
400g/14 oz canned black cherries, pitted
2 × 15ml spoons/2 tablespoons black cherry jam
juice of 1 orange
2 × 5ml spoons/2 teaspoons cornflour
2 × 15ml spoons/2 tablespoons brandy

Cook the lumache in a large pan of steadily boiling water until *al dente* with the olive oil and salt.

Meanwhile, drain the cherries and put their juice into a pan. Add the jam to the cherry juice and stir over gentle heat until the jam has dissolved. Blend the orange juice and cornflour to a smooth paste, and stir in a little of the hot cherry liquid. Return to the remaining juice in the pan, and stir over gentle heat until the cherry juice thickens. Stir in the brandy.

Drain the cooked pasta thoroughly and transfer to a serving dish. Spoon the hot cherry sauce over the top and serve immediately with whipped cream or ice cream.

PASTA WITH FUDGE SAUCE

225g/8 oz fettucine
1 × 15ml spoon/1 tablespoon olive oil
1 × 5ml spoon/1 teaspoon salt
75g/3 oz butter
75g/3 oz soft brown sugar
100g/4 oz chopped marshmallows
3 × 15ml spoons/3 tablespoons double cream
a few drops butterscotch essence

Cook the fettucine in a large pan of steadily boiling water until *al dente* with the olive oil and salt.

Meanwhile, put the butter, sugar, marshmallows and cream into a pan, and stir over gentle heat until melted. Add butterscotch essence to taste.

Drain the cooked fettucine thoroughly and transfer to a serving dish. Spoon the hot fudge sauce over the top and serve immediately.

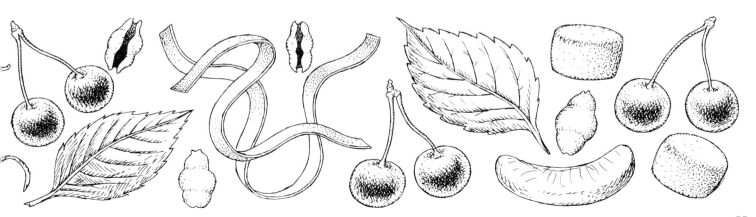

FRESH FIG AND PASTA PUDDING

8 fresh figs, chopped
4 × 15ml spoons/4 tablespoons Maraschino liqueur
225g/8 oz farfalle (pasta bows)
1 × 15ml spoon/1 tablespoon olive oil
1 × 5ml spoon/1 teaspoon salt
175g/6 oz fresh raspberries
50g/2 oz Amaretti (small macaroons), finely crumbled
150ml/¼ pint double cream, lightly whipped

DECORATION
crumbled Amaretti

Put the figs into a bowl with the Maraschino liqueur; cover and chill for 1 hour.

Meanwhile, cook the farfalle in a large pan of steadily boiling water until *al dente* with the oil and salt.

Sieve the fresh raspberries and mix with the crumbled Amaretti and the double cream. Stir in the chilled figs and their juices.

Drain the pasta thoroughly, reserve four bows and transfer the rest to individual serving dishes. Top each dish with the prepared fruit and cream sauce, decorate with the crumbled Amaretti and reserved pasta bows, and serve immediately.

BANANA BOWS

225g/8 oz farfalle (pasta bows)
1 × 15ml spoon/1 tablespoon olive oil
1 × 5ml spoon/1 teaspoon salt
225g/8 oz clear honey
grated rind and juice of 2 lemons
100g/4 oz raisins
50g/2 oz glacé cherries, chopped
50g/2 oz butter
2 bananas, cut into diagonal slices

Cook the farfalle in a large pan of steadily boiling water until *al dente* with the oil and salt.

Meanwhile, heat the honey, lemon rind and juice, the raisins and chopped cherries in a pan.

Melt the butter in a clean pan and fry the sliced banana for 2–3 minutes until lightly golden.

Drain the pasta thoroughly, then gently stir in the hot honey sauce and the fried banana. Transfer to a serving dish and serve immediately.

Fresh Fig and Pasta Pudding